# Craftsmen at Work

# CRAFTSMEN AT WORK

JOHN NORWOOD

JOHN BAKER · LONDON

First published 1977
John Baker (Publishers) Ltd
35 Bedford Row, London WC1R 4JH

© John Norwood, 1977

ISBN 0 212 97019 4

Printed in Great Britain by
Hollen Street Press Ltd at Slough, Berkshire

To Pamela

# Contents

## SURVIVING CRAFTS

## VANISHED CRAFTS

# Introduction

'I like work,' wrote Jerome K. Jerome. 'It fascinates me. I can sit and look at it for hours.' And while I admit to sharing the same fascination, I would not like the reader to think it was the only reason this book came to be written; actually, it was the outcome of a survey intended to discover what crafts survived in one English county, and how they were being carried on. It began with the rather premature assumption that there could be very few traditional craftsmen still at work, and some record of them should therefore be made before it was too late; but as it turned out, a surprising number came to light and it is quite possible that further search would have produced even more. There is no reason to suppose from this, however, that Hampshire is more remarkable than many other counties for the number of its active crafts, which seems to point to the survival of a considerable resource of traditional hand skills. It also offers some reassurance to those who fear that the old values associated with such skills have gone for good.

Intent on such a search, one soon observes how the word 'craft' means different things to different people. To some it implies the pursuit of a hobby with a certain degree of dexterity; to others, almost any kind of rural labour, usually close to extinction and quaint withal; while there are those who apply the word primarily to certain kinds of artistic expression, often known as 'creative crafts'. Then again, the term 'craftsman' is often used as a compliment to someone who has done a good piece of work, whether it be overhauling an engine, writing a report or growing a row of onions. In fact, the word tends to be used pretty loosely of those who work at uncommon trades, or do their jobs particularly well, or carry on into ripe old age.

So what is it that the people whose work is described in these pages have in common? Quite simply, they all make things by hand: which for most purposes is a passable definition of a craftsman, even though much ink has been used in categorising the qualities he ought to possess. It is only necessary to add that a craftsman has a personal influence on the form of each thing he makes, and this distinguishes him from say, a machine setter working (with undoubted skill) to produce a series of identical objects. Thus, the handmade thing has a subtle quality that defies imitation; as one of the craftsmen in these pages said, attempting to evaluate his work, 'It's got the mark of humanity on it.' Another quoted to me D. H. Lawrence's lines 'Things men have made' to illustrate his conviction that such objects may embody a kind of continuing vitality. Most craftsmen are less articulate than these two but would probably give a nod to the general idea. What makes a craftsman a good one is a more subjective consideration altogether, but a guide to the answer may be found in Bernard Leach's definition of craft: *Good work proceeding from the whole man; heart, head and hand in proper balance.* (Quoted in Soetsu Yanagi: *The Unknown Craftsman*, Tokyo 1972, p.95.)

All of the crafts described (save those in the last chapter) were found in an active state, though admittedly one or two were only just; all of them were, or had been, carried on as a means of livelihood; and all were producing functional goods. To my surprise, four or five had not apparently been described before. The list should not, of course, be regarded as anything like a full one, even for southern England, but it is long enough to be divided into certain significant categories.

First then, is the group I refer to as *Enduring Crafts*, because they are meeting a continuing demand and no other way of doing the job is likely to be devised. (We could reasonably include some of the sporting crafts among them: could one imagine any mechanism capable of shoeing a racehorse?) The market for these skills is appreciably smaller than it once was, but for some of them at least it looks as though they have found a natural level where they will remain steady. Take as an example the blacksmiths, now much depleted in number because modern agriculture and transport no longer depend on the village forge; for all that, we can safely look into the future and predict the continuing need for a hundred and one pieces of metal still to be shaped, sharpened or repaired at their hands.

The second group, comprising the *Sporting Crafts* and the *Design Crafts* is the flourishing one. (This, of course, is also true of some of the crafts in the first group.) It is interesting to see how the increased leisure and expanded recreational facilities many of us now enjoy have made new opportunities for some workers who not so long ago might have been in danger of going out of business. At the same time, there seems to be a growing appreciation of well-designed handwork for which a good many people are prepared to pay, and this is certainly to the advantage of those crafts with aesthetic appeal. The generally healthy condition of this whole group should serve as a corrective to those who bewail the apparent death of craftsmanship, and show the common sense of looking for it where a need exists to be served.

Thirdly, there are those crafts at their last gasp, the *Surviving Crafts*, whose practitioners are to be reckoned alone or at best in handfuls. I use the term survivors in the sense of those lingering on after their due time, for it seems doubtful if they will ever again meet a real, widespread need; though a few may be found here and there for years yet, or may continue, like the wheelwright, to serve a highly specialised market. The decline of those crafts serving basically rural needs, sad though it is, only reflects the changes that have taken place in the countryside over the last thirty or forty years, particularly increased mechanisation and the departure of the former rural population. As an example of the way recently-familiar things are disappearing before our very eyes, it gave me particular regret that despite looking far and wide I failed to find a single hedge layer active in the area of the survey.

In the course of watching and listening to craftsmen I have enjoyed many opportunities of learning not only how they go about their work but what they feel about it – some illuminating indications of those feelings will be found here and there in the book. I venture also a few generalisations on the craftsman's qualities and values in the hope that they may lead to a fuller understanding and appreciation of his way of life.

One of the first things usually to become apparent is a respect for the tools and materials of the trade. Tools are the extension of the worker's hands and their capabilities are as familiar to him as their feel; they are his daily companions, often treasured as they were by his father before him. He has a similar intimacy with the material he works in and a critical appreciation of its quality. Whatever it is – wood, leather, stone or cloth – nothing pleases him better than to have 'good stuff' to work with, and he knows to an inch what it is capable of. Men who thus handle, shape and transform materials are often deeply contented, for they have a relationship with the enduring physical world. George Sturt had seen the truth of this when he wrote:

> No higher wage, no income will buy for men that satisfaction which of old – until machinery made drudges of them – streamed into their muscles all day long from close contact with iron, timber, clay, wind and wave, horse-strength. It tingled up in the niceties of touch, sight, scent. The very ears unawares received it, as when the plane went singing over the wood, or the exact chisel went tapping in (under the mallet) to the hard ash with gentle sound. But these intimacies are over. Although they have so much more leisure men can now taste little solace in life, of the sort that skilled hand-work used to yield to them. (*The Wheelwright's Shop*, 1923, ch.37.)

No less obvious is a real concern for quality of workmanship, something I heard expressed many times (even when it seemed that only another craftsman could be capable of judging). True, making things by hand is no guarantee that they will be well made, and poor goods are sometimes met with, but I am inclined to think that an urge to work to a high standard is part of the craftsman's essential integrity. 'I don't concern myself with how long it takes; it's how well it's done,' said one of my informants, showing a healthy lack of respect for the factor which most other workers think so important.

Further characteristics of craftsmen as a breed are that they are hard-working and independent, both traits probably owing something to self-employment and the mastery of specialised skills. With the independence there is sometimes linked a sense of isolation that may indeed arise from increasing rarity of a particular occupation. While pride in their work is never far from the surface, neither is a realism born of the struggle to acquire proficiency and become established, to overcome shortages and make ends meet. I am sceptical about those who make romantic claims for the craftsman's way of life since they rarely ring true – and let it be noted that the very word craft is strange to many a worker who generally refers to his job as a trade.

The worth of such attitudes to work does not need to be emphasised: they throw into sad contrast the dreary, impersonal, unfulfilling nature of employment for huge numbers of people.

There is one last point that ought to be made. Some books on crafts – and perhaps this one – give the impression that there is an orthodox way of doing things and a standard nomenclature for tools and processes; that is not often so. With the rural crafts especially there may be great variation from one part of the country to another, even from one worker to the next, and the names used, as well as the things done, may differ considerably from any printed description. Such variability is part of the richness of the subject, and often springs from the ingenuity of individuals in finding their own way of tackling a problem or improving their methods. What I have attempted in these pages is to describe things as I found them rather than to draw an 'ideal' picture of any craft; and while this occasionally means recording some practice that might have been looked at askance by a previous generation, it is nevertheless an account of the work of real people in actual situations. Most of what is described I have seen with my own eyes, with the exception of certain stages of the more complex crafts which the limitations of time or opportunity denied me. The conversational extracts are given verbatim.

I hope that readers will find themselves sharing something of my own pleasure in the discovery of this fascinating range of skills. It is heightened for me by recollection of the circumstances of discovery: in large workshops or small workrooms, some crowded with the clutter of the years, others tidy and businesslike; in the sounds of fabrication and the scent of materials, often evocative of a whole way of life; and in conversations rich with anecdote and cherished wisdom. These things I shall long remember, like the personalities of the men and women whose work is dealt with. This book is really a tribute to them, for without them it could not have been written.

# Acknowledgements

It gives me great pleasure to acknowledge my indebtedness to the following for their help in the preparation of this book:

First and foremost, to the men and women whose work is described and whom it has been a privilege to know. With invariable courtesy they made me welcome in their workshops and homes, and were generous in explaining their work, demonstrating their methods, and answering my questions. Several helped yet further by reading chapters in draft form and making many useful amendments.

To the following firms who readily co-operated in allowing me the freedom of their premises and making facilities available:
    Alresford Saddlers Ltd. (New Alresford)
    Berthon Boat Company Ltd. (Lymington)
    Blackwell and Moody, Stonemasons (Winchester)
    Butler, Verner, Sailmakers (Gosport)
    East Bros. (Timber) Ltd. (West Dean)
    Michelmersh Brick and Tile Company Ltd. (Romsey)
    J. Salter and Son, Polo Specialists (Aldershot)
    Yateley Industries for Disabled Girls, Textile Printers (Yateley)

To Hampshire County Museum Service, Winchester, under whose auspices the survey was made on which the book is based, for permission to quote original source material and to reproduce most of the photographs; and to Miss Margaret Macfarlane, former Director of the Service, for her encouragement at all stages.

To the Council for Small Industries in Rural Areas, for permission to reproduce the photographs on pages 145 and 147; and to Mr Derek Joseph for his skill in copying the remaining photographs from transparencies taken by the author.

*Acknowledgements*

To the staff of the reference departments of Hampshire County Library, Winchester, and West Sussex County Library, Worthing, for their effective help in pursuing numerous enquiries.

To my wife, for bearing many inconveniences generously during the book's gestation, and particularly for typing the manuscript; and to my father for his helpful comments made in the course of looking over the draft chapters.

NOTE
Changes are bound to occur in the time that elapses between writing about the work of a craftsman and the appearance of that account in print. The circumstances of one or two individuals have altered to my knowledge, but it seems best to leave the record as I found it, trusting that those concerned will accept it as a fair account of things as they were.

# ENDURING CRAFTS

# The basket maker

For a number of reasons we can look at basket making as a classic craft, occupying a position typical of the crafts in today's world; and we can also look at the subject of this chapter, Jim Tongs of Southampton, in the same light. For he is typical of the craftsmen who are managing to survive in an industrialised society, in which it might seem the odds were against them and the pressures intolerable.

To begin with, basket making has a long history: and not just a respectable old age, but a very great antiquity. A sizeable part of a small basket was found during excavation of the Romano-British town of Silchester, and earlier fragments datable to the second century BC were recovered from the lake village at Glastonbury in Somerset. This seems to be the oldest wicker basket known in Britain, but there is evidence that coiled baskets, made of vegetable fibres sewn together in a continuous spiral, are as old as the New Stone Age. It has been argued that the earliest coil-made pottery was derived from this technique, which would put basketry among the most ancient hand crafts known to man.

The craft depends upon a regular supply of the right quality of raw material, in this case young growths or *rods*, usually of the Almond Willow, *Salix triandra*. (In other parts of the world many different kinds of twigs, stalks, roots, canes and fibres are put to use.) All English willow comes from Somerset, where it can be seen growing in dense blocks on the flat alluvial moors; the laborious processes of cultivation and preparation would make a story in themselves. Willows used also to be grown in parts of the Midlands, Lancashire and East Anglia, and in small patches of suitable land in other areas, but it is doubtful whether more than a minute quantity has been harvested outside Somerset for many years. A good deal is imported, and several kinds of Far-Eastern cane are used extensively in basket making, chiefly of the more ornamental sort. *Centre cane*, the creamy fibrous core that is left when the outer casing has been stripped off, is

*Both hands and a foot are needed when making the slath, or foundation, of a circular basket. The sticks are pared down to reduce bulk and four of them are pierced for the others to pass through. An additional half-stick is inserted to avoid the weave repeating, as it would do on an even number.*

popular with schools and hobbyists as it is available in regular dimensions and is easy to manipulate.

Basketry, in common with many other crafts, has gone into a severe decline in the years since the Second World War. One reason is the massive growth of alternative forms of containers and packaging, another is the endless supply of cheap goods from·the Canary Isles and the Far East. English basket makers have found it very difficult to remain competitive and a great many have not survived. And, on top of these problems, has been the reluctance of youngsters to take up the less rewarding hand work when more lucrative opportunities abound.

Yet, despite all the difficulties, basket making seems likely to survive. Its products are hard-wearing, strong for weight, resilient, repairable, good looking and readily adaptable to all sorts of requirements. Basketry will

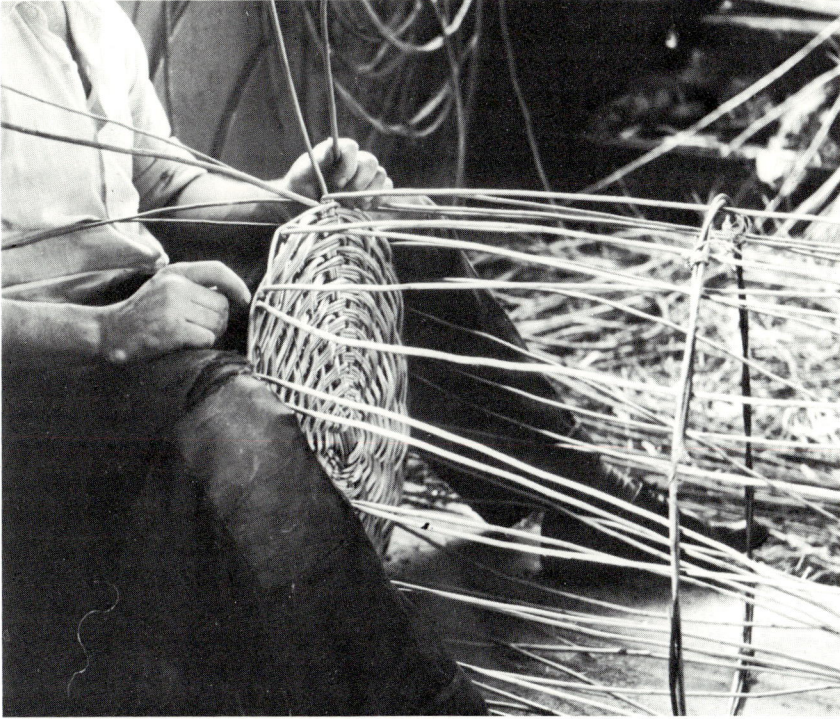

*When the base is made, stakes are pushed in on each side of every bottom stick and bent up to form the skeleton of the sides; a willow hoop keeps the long whippy ends out of the way.*

probably always be preferred for a wide range of uses, and, of course, it is impossible to make by machine. Mr Tongs is not slow to see where that leaves him. 'While we're getting scarce', he points out, 'there's a future for basket makers.' It is a paradox applicable to many an old specialised trade.

Mr Tongs is a third-generation craftsman, something one comes across quite often. The business began over a century ago and consisted of a shop and workroom near the docks, a good situation in those days as much work was done for the shipping lines. Three or four men were employed. There must have been a considerable pressure of work at times, for Mr Tongs' father used to recount how he shared with his ten brothers and sisters the tedious work of mending ships' chairs (cane seating usually goes with basket making). Since the war, redevelopment of the older parts of Southampton has meant three moves for the little firm and Mr Tongs now works on his own in a spacious garage at the end of his garden in Bitterne; the former retail trade has more or less been given up but goods are made to order and sold to shops as far away as Surrey.

An important aspect of willow growing is the preparation of the different kinds of rods. *Green willow*, used as cut, without preparation, is used only rarely, for cheap outdoor baskets, and never by Mr Tongs. The two kinds in commonest use are *buff willow* and *white willow*. Rods for the former are boiled for seven or eight hours in huge tanks and left to soak for another twenty-four, so that the bark can stain the wood a warm golden-brown; then they are stripped and thoroughly dried in the open air. Rods for white willow are cut during the winter months and *pitted*, or stood in shallow pits of water, for eight to twelve weeks until, with the rising sap of spring they start to break into leaf; stripping then reveals the clean white rods. Baskets made of white willow are extensively used in the catering trades, and the white rods can be used to achieve a pleasant contrast with buff and brown. *Brown willow*, well dried outdoors before use and with the bark left on, is in limited demand for agricultural baskets. Willow is supplied to the maker in bundles of 37 in circumference just above the base, and in lengths ranging from 3 ft – 9 ft.

Before Mr Tongs can begin to use his rods he must bring them to the right condition by dampening. Small ones may be all right after an hour's soaking but larger ones will need steeping overnight – so he has to think ahead about the day's work or there may not be enough rods to get on with. During the day they are kept moist under a damp sack.

Basket makers work on the floor. Mr Tongs seats himself on a panel of planking, back to the wall, with the rods to hand on his right, under their sacking. Most of the work is done on a *lap board*, a plank panel about 21 in × 30 in, raised at the nearer end so that the side of the basket being made is kept in view; the board rests across the thighs. On mild days Mr Tongs sits with the doors open and puts out a range of baskets on the low roof. As the day wears on, the sun shines in on the bundles of rods, stacks of baskets and chairs for caning, and draws out the mellow fragrance of the willows. The workshop doors face the pavement and curious passers-by and children on their way home from school look in to see a 'real basket maker' at work.

Circular baskets are begun in the following way, with modification for oval shapes: eight stout rods, known as the *sticks*, are selected as the main members of the base and cut about 2 in longer than the intended diameter (say, 20 in for an 18 in basket). Their thickness is pared down in the middle with a knife and four are pierced at the centre; through these, the other four are passed and the ends spread out star-like. They are secured by binding round with a rod or two, and an additional half-length stick is

*A dog basket (turned out in some numbers by most basket makers) nears completion. The side stakes are being bent over and plaited to form a strong, integral border.*

inserted at one side – the strongest kind of base is worked round an uneven number of sticks. This structure is called the *slath* and it is made on the floor, using a foot to keep it steady. The base is completed by weaving round to the required diameter and trimming off the sticks. More strong rods are now selected for the uprights or *stakes* and one is thrust well into the weave on both sides of every bottom stick, so doubling their number. At the circumference they are bent up over the edge of a knife blade.

The first few courses of the sides are strongly and carefully worked as this *upsett* will determine the basket's symmetry. The ends of the stakes are long and whippy, so Mr Tongs slips a willow hoop over them to keep them under control as he begins weaving upwards, using the *strokes* appropriate to the function of the basket or the decorative effect he is after. Basket makers work in an anti-clockwise direction, keeping the basket steady with a lead weight placed inside and taking care that as the sides rise the weave is tight and level. A heavy *beating iron* can be used to pack it down; the tool is often ring-ended to double as a *commander* for straightening very thick rods. When the top is reached, the border may be worked in various ways: *scallop*, a hooped top; *trac*, which is a simple tucking-in of the rod ends; *plain*, which produces a narrow flat top; and *plait*, which produces a broad flat top with the addition of extra stakes. By using the stakes to form the border the basket sides are both reinforced and made absolutely secure. A handle is fitted to many baskets, consisting of a stout willow *bow* with ends pared, or *slyped*, to insert into the edge of the weave, bound and secured with fine rods, split cane or split willow *skeins*. (Space is allowed for the bow when working the border by letting in a temporary *bow-mark* of the same diameter.) The finishing touch is given to a basket by trimming off all projecting ends with the *picking knife*, whose wedge-shaped blade is handy for getting into awkward corners; this ancient tool appears on the arms of the Basketmakers' Company.

As a good many rectangular baskets are made for various purposes (laundry baskets, bottle baskets, airborne panniers) a different technique has to be used for making their bases. This requires a *clamp* of wood adjusted by two screws which will hold a set of sticks while a panel is woven; when this is removed from the clamp, stakes are inserted along each edge and an upsett worked as before, except, of course, that the sides are straight. Extra stout stakes are often used to strengthen the corners of large hampers and to form legs or hinge bars in other baskets, and Mr Tongs keeps a pair of *croppers* for cutting them. When willow has to be split for some purpose such as the handle binding mentioned above, a curious tool called a *cleaver* is used, which is an egg-shaped piece of box-wood with four fins; the willow is given a cross cut on the end and then forced against the fins to open the splits. The pith attached is removed with a *shave*, a small block-like tool with a blade in one face and an adjustable platform to regulate thickness.

One or two other basket making tools may also be mentioned. A *shop knife* is used for general trimming and slyping work; *bodkins* of various sizes, lubricated with a *grease horn* are used to make openings in the weave when rods have to be inserted; an *under-putter* has a hollowed, curved blade used to guide an inserted rod back into the weave when repairing a basket too big to get the other hand inside; and, by no means least important, there is the *measuring rod*, a 3 ft length of willow marked with brass pins at every inch and three inches and at twelve, eighteen and twenty-four inches. The whole tool kit is quite a simple one – and it has even been said that it would be possible for a basket maker to work with nothing more than a knife.

Although somewhat limited in his range of materials, the basket maker can ring many changes with his choice of strokes, using them for both decorative and functional effect. *Randing* is the most basic stroke of all,

Tools of the basket maker's trade, seen resting on a well-used lap board.
*(1) Mallet (2) Measuring rod (3) Cleaver: splits rods for fine work (4) Shave: trims split rods (5-7) Bodkins: open the weave (8) Grease horn: lubricates bodkins (9) Under-putter: guides rods in repair work (10) Shop knife (11) Picking knife: trims off ends when finishing (12) Croppers: cut large stakes (13) Lead weight: keeps work steady (14) Beating iron/commander: blade beats work down, ring straightens bent stakes (15) Hoop: keeps ends of stakes under control.*

one rod woven in and out of every stake; in *slewing* two or more rods are worked together; *fitching* is working two rods alternately in and out and over and under each other – reversed, it is *pairing* and both achieve a tight grip; *waling* is three or more rods worked alternately in front of two or more stakes and behind one. Some strokes are slower than others and so make for a more expensive basket, others may be useful where a light-weight job is required – for example, in the case of the huge baskets Mr Tongs makes for a local wastepaper works, in which he leaves large areas of open-work, held tightly with fitching.

Jim Tongs will turn his hand to making any kind of basket he is asked for and there is usually an interesting range to be seen awaiting collection from the workshop: baskets for butchers and bakers, for shopping and gardening, for logs, laundry and firehoses; he will make babies' cradles and children's chairs and the traditional baskets carried by gipsy flower sellers. One of the steadiest demands – as one might expect from a nation of pet-lovers – is for dog and cat baskets, the latter made with a cosy hood, looking for all the world like some sort of feline bird's-nest. Such is the adaptability of the useful willow, combined with the ingenious skill of the basket maker.

# The blacksmith

Legend and literature hold the blacksmith in greater esteem than all other craftsmen, and it is hardly an exaggeration to claim that he is one of the makers of civilization as we know it. Most of the modern industries which involve metal fabrication can count themselves in the direct line of descent from the metalworkers of prehistoric times, by way of those specialists who appeared on the scene as need arose: armourers and gun makers, clock and instrument makers, sheet metal workers and machinery builders. Throughout history the workers in metal have been among the most highly skilled of tradesmen, making the tools and equipment for most of the others; and we can imagine the awe in which primitive people held the man who could control fire and bring out of it a new and marvellous material. The blacksmith of today has a common kinship with metalworkers all down the long corridors of time, yet he himself remains essentially what he has always been, a servant of other trades. The old motto of the Black-smiths' Company is by no means out of date when it asserts: *By hammer and hand all arts do stand.*

Some people think of the blacksmith in other terms. To many, he is first and foremost the man who shoes horses, and until recently this has nearly always been one of his principal occupations; the very name for this aspect of his work, farriery, derives from the Latin for iron, *ferrum*. But today it is often the case that the smith does not handle horses at all, for, with the decline in the horse population, shoeing has tended to become the province of a relatively small number of men willing to undergo additional training and acquire the necessary skill. There are others for whom blacksmithing means the making of decorative wrought iron work such as gates, balconies, firebaskets and the like, and who cherish the image of the smith as a creative worker; and it is good to know that some of them do indeed concentrate on this kind of work and have acquired a high reputation for it. CoSIRA, the Council for Small Industries in Rural Areas, has made a laudable effort through its training schemes and publications to encourage blacksmiths to apply imagination as well as skill to their work, and it is noticeable that much handmade ironwork, even of quite humble use, has a distinctly decorative quality.

Setting aside these two rather specialised aspects of the craft, what place is there today for the old-fashioned, all-purpose blacksmith? One may even be driven to ask if he actually survives, for he is noticeably more difficult to find than he used to be, and the countryside is dotted with once-busy smithies now transmogrified into Old Forge Cottages. The observant traveller will notice such tell-tale signs of former forges as little buildings with wide double doors, squat smoke-blackened chimneys and low side windows, with perhaps a huge iron tyring platform lying over-grown nearby. More forges are to be found concealed behind the fronts of older garages, for the motor car was the chief factor in the decline of the blacksmith's trade; countless smiths, like the one portrayed in Stan Merritt's lines, must have seized their chance to make the best of a bad job:

> Beneath a huge electric sign,
> The village smith now sits;
> His brawny form, though plump and fat,
> His easy chair just fits.

> The old clay pipe is laid away,
> His brow reveals no sweat;
> He calmly views the cars roll up
> And puffs a cigarette.

> Six shining pumps adorn the spot
> Where once the anvil stood:
> The heavy traffic daily pays
> This modern Robin Hood.

That was written in 1911. However, if you search for him the blacksmith is still to be met with, fulfilling the age-old function of giving service to other sections of the working community; he may carry out some shoeing and he may find time to do some decorative work, but the probability is that most of his energies are given to jobbing work. Perhaps that does not sound very significant, yet it implies a daily challenge to his ability and ingenuity and also involvement in the problems of all kinds of people. Consider some of the things that Steve Pibworth of Petersfield dealt with in a typical week's work.

He made: twelve angle brackets for a builder and twelve stakes for a gardener; more brackets for a horse box and a church monument; a set of bars for a bank window; frames for a mat well and a manhole cover. He

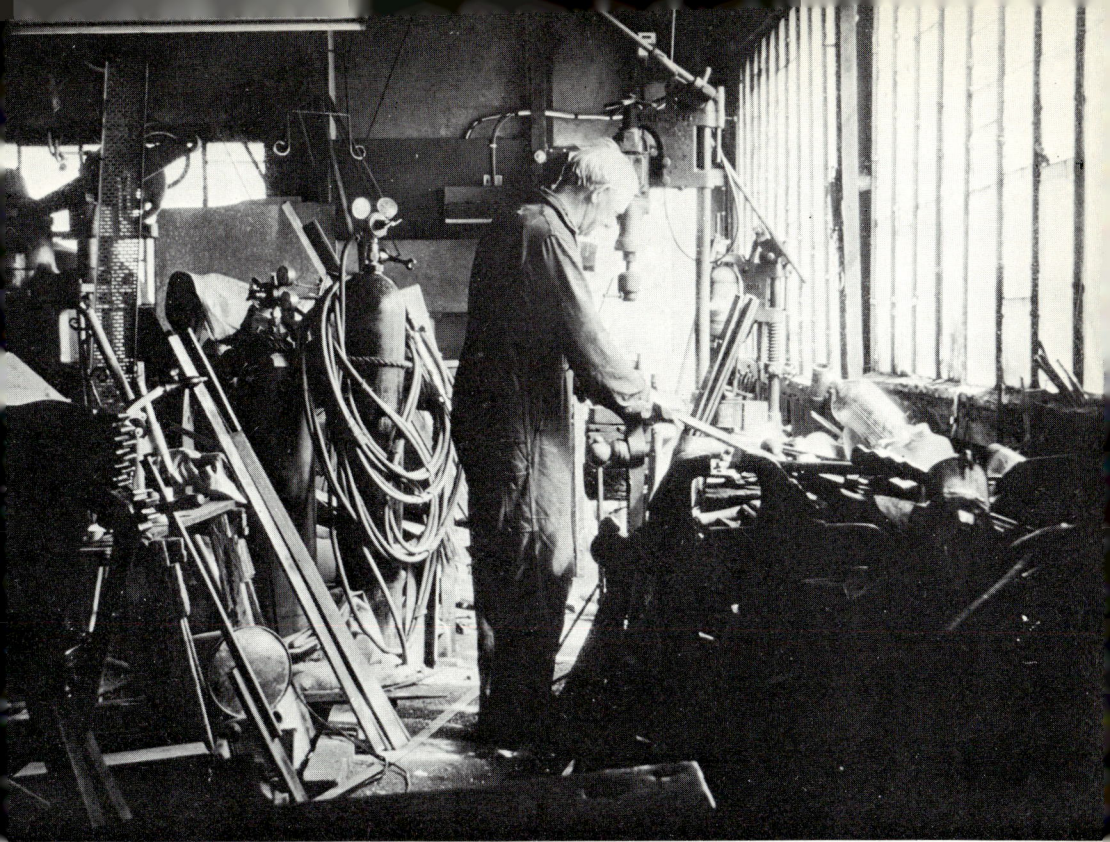

*While the inside of a forge may look chaotic to a stranger, the blacksmith has a pretty good idea of where everything is. The windows with their over-lapping panes indicate a workshop of some age, but power tools and oxy-acetylene gear show that techniques are up to date.*

straightened the tines of a loader for one farmer and made a set of large staples for another; straightened the hand of a church clock; worked out an estimate for making a handrail for a hospital ramp; and supplied numerous nuts and bolts and cut lengths of steel to a variety of customers. He also found time to complete his main job of the week, making a 20 ft decorative fitment for a pub bar. This list is enough to show that the old versatility of the blacksmith has been carried forward into modern times and that he is just as indispensable as he ever was. Of course, many agricultural repair jobs are carried out by machinery dealers, and a number of farmers are ready to attempt their own welding repairs, but when real understanding is needed it is good to have the blacksmith to rely on. Mr Pibworth is not dissatisfied with the situation and knows his work will always be in demand one way or another: 'If there's a boom on, then they have everything new; if things are tight then they have the things repaired. You're onto a winner whatever's happening!'

Mr Pibworth manages to look quite unlike Longfellow's stereotype of the village blacksmith, nor does he have the background of one. He was a grammar school boy who came to blacksmithing almost by accident when his father heard that a local smith needed an assistant and thought it would suit him. It did, and he stayed 'just picking it up'; he served no formal apprenticeship. As to the brawn, he believes that acquired knack and application of intelligence are to a large extent an effective substitute; patience, too, is an asset.

In the fullness of time, the old blacksmith retired and Mr Pibworth was able to carry on the business. For perhaps 150 years it has stood at a busy crossroads only a short way from the centre of the town, a position that in the horse age must have been a particularly good one. Today it consists of three buildings. The main one contains the hearth and anvil, and has a long bench under the window with leg vices and sundry power tools. It also houses what the ignorant might consider an unbelievable clutter of old iron, but is in fact a mixture of things waiting to be fixed, things waiting to be collected, interesting things that Mr Pibworth may find a sale for, and bits and pieces that are bound to come in useful sometime. He knows just where they all are. Adjoining it is another building used chiefly for constructional work, where there are two steel benches, power saws and welding gear (two arc welders and an oxy-acetylene set). Here also are racks for the stock of small steel sections. The third shed is the stores, neatly organised and labelled, from which Mr Pibworth is able to supply a wide range of nuts, bolts and metal fittings. He reckons to be something of a steel stockholder as well, so the small forecourt is crammed with girder lengths, the longer ones partly accommodated by being passed through a hole cut in the wall of one building. The same forecourt does duty as a work area for larger jobs, and Mr Pibworth or one of his helpers is often to be seen out there repairing some unwieldy object like a harrow or an excavator bucket. The helpers consist of a pensioner who has had a lifetime in engineering and can turn his hand to anything, a lad who is thought by the boss to show real promise, and a part-timer who comes in to assist generally. They work together in the harmonious way characteristic of blacksmiths' shops, where good understanding is a vital part of handling hot metal quickly and efficiently.

The heart of the shop is, of course, the hearth. Here, it is of modern steel construction and consists basically of a deep tray in which the fire is built up, into which projects the nozzle or *tue iron* of an electric blower. In front is the *bosh*, a water trough used for cooling metal and tempering tools; overhead is a smoke canopy. Mr Pibworth uses three tools to control his fire: poker, *slice* (flat shovel) and *swab* for wetting and retarding it. Management of the fire is quite an art and depends a lot on the fuel available; ideally it should be easy to light, give good heat and neither flare up

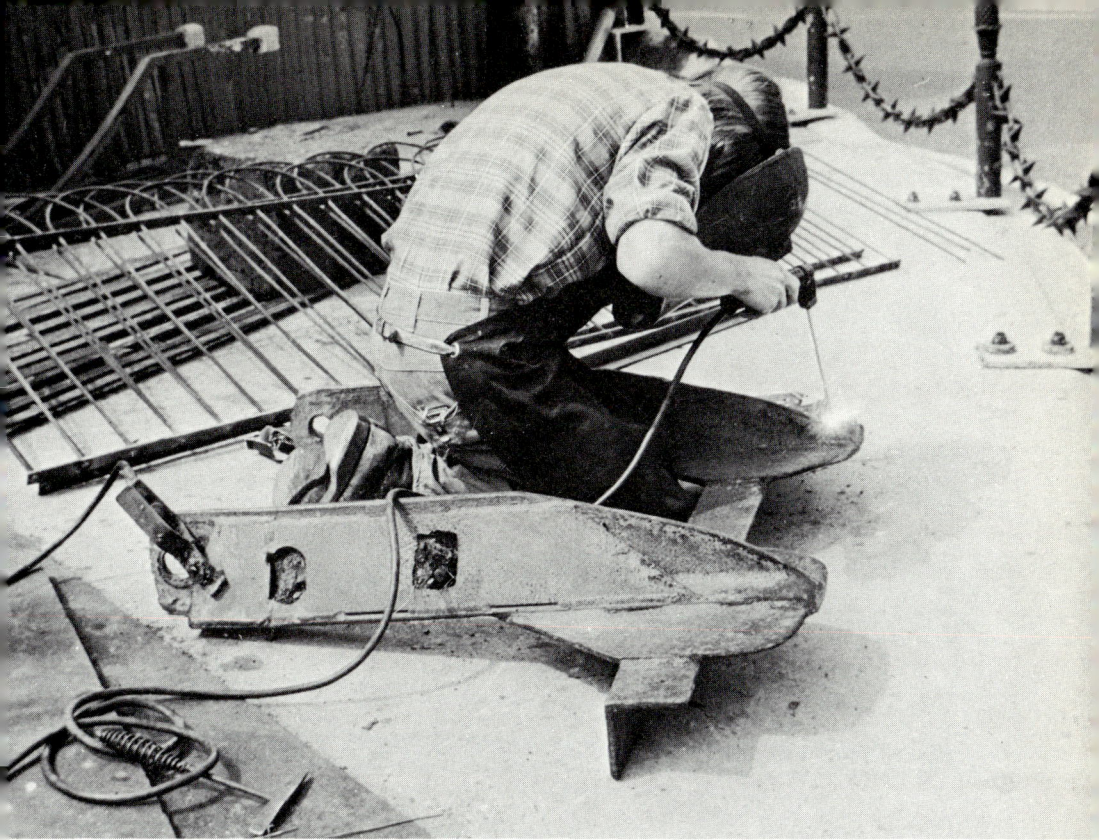

*The blacksmith's assistant repairs an excavator jaw with an electric arc welder; on the ground behind him is a scaling hammer to be used for cleaning up the weld. The forecourt of the forge is on one corner of a busy crossroads.*

nor readily form clinker. Close to the hearth stands the anvil. The pointed *bick* end would normally be to the user's right, but as Mr Pibworth happens to be left-handed it stands the other way round. All sorts of curved work is done on the bick. The long top is the *face*, and on its *hanging end* are a round *punching hole* and a square *hardie hole* in which certain tools can be held. Between the face and the bick is a *table* of un-hardened steel on which cutting is done to avoid damaging tool edges. The customary way of mounting an anvil is on a length of tree trunk set in the floor, but this, although it allows excellent spring when hammering, has the disadvantage of immobility and Mr Pibworth uses a steel stand.

Hammers are the tools most often in the blacksmith's hand. Mr Pibworth uses four regularly and another fifteen or sixteen from time to time. Every smith knows the feel of his favourite hammer – it becomes an extension of his working arm and he is uncomfortable if he has to make do without it. Next most frequently he uses *tongs*. Not just a pair of tongs, but a great number of them. It is of great importance for the smith to be able to grip and turn his workpiece easily and he will regularly make pairs of tongs for

29

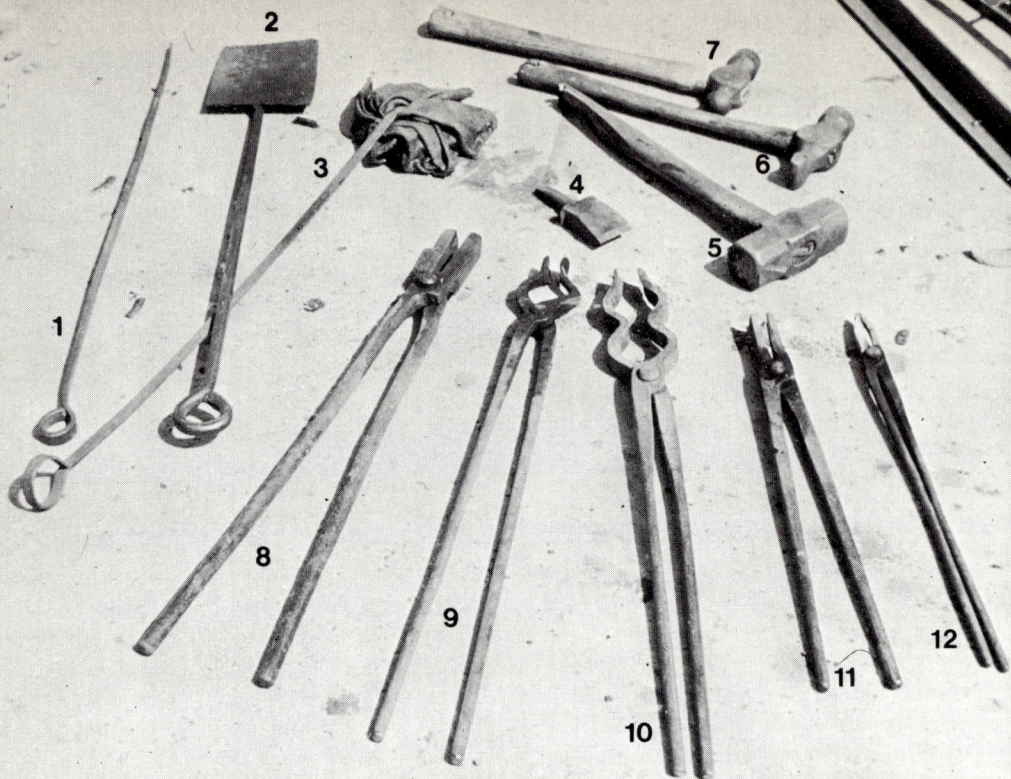

*Some of the blacksmith's most frequently-used tools.*
*(1) Poker (2) Slice, and (3) Swab: used to control the fire (4) Hardie: fitted*
*into a hole in the anvil for cutting metal on (5) Sledge (6) Cross pane, and*
*(7) Ball pane hammers: these are almost part of the smith's right hand (8-12)*
*Tongs: usually made as required.*

special uses. He also needs a range of *cold chisels* (short and stout) and *hot chisels* (long and slender) for use with a hand hammer when cutting iron, and *cold sets* and *hot sets* of similar proportion for use with a sledge hammer; they are either hafted, or have a grooved waist by which they are held with a long rod twisted round them. Of like function are *hardies*, fitted into the square hole of the anvil, onto which bars may be hammered to cut them.

Several kinds of tool help the blacksmith with his shaping operations. *Swages* are paired tools between which metal lengths are worked; the bottom one fits into the hardie hole and the top one, held by a twisted rod, is struck with the sledge hammer. *Fullers*, like thick rounded chisels, are used for working shoulders and indentations and may be used singly or in pairs like swages. *Flatters* can be hafted or rodded, with flat or convex faces, and are used for putting a smooth surface on newly forged work, as their name implies. These days, with so many jobs being made up in mild steel, they do not get the use they once did when fire forging and welding predominated, and Mr Pibworth, to his disgust, has actually had customers asking for hammer marks to be shown on their work as proof that it is handmade!

Two large items that will be found somewhere on the floor of every blacksmith's shop are a *cone mandrel*, and a *swage block*. The first, a heavy iron cone about 4 ft tall, is employed when trueing-up rings and circular pieces; the second is a thick rectangular iron block pierced with a variety of square and round holes, and with many sizes of half-round and V notches on its sides, in which metal can be shaped by hammering. These are all tools which the smith has used for centuries, to which, as already indicated, a number of important additions have been made. Mr Pibworth has several electric drills of chuck capacity from ¼ in to 1 in, a variety of grinders and wire brushes, bending roll for sheet metal work, hydraulic pipe bender, planishing machine, and his welders.

The scarcity of wrought iron and the preponderance of mild steel are the two factors which have caused the biggest change in the smith's methods in recent years. Gas and electric welding of steel are much easier than fire welding, and there is not a great deal of old-fashioned forging being done in Mr Pibworth's shop. 'If it's done intelligently', he claims, 'the finished product can look just as good as if it's done in the fire. It's quite amazing what one can do with the oxy-acetylene cutter combined with the arc welder: you can make shapes and forms that in the old days you'd never dream of being able to do.'

Nevertheless, the blacksmith still needs a thorough grounding in the basic techniques of working metal. They are six in number: *drawing down* is reducing the thickness of a piece of metal by hammering, so lengthening or widening it, and is done either on the anvil or between a pair of fullers; *upsetting* (or *jumping up*) means increasing thickness by hammering or beating the end of the metal so that a heated part swells; *bending*, largely used in decorative scroll work (with the aid of special scroll tools) is best done hot, taking care to avoid stretching on the outer curve; *punching* makes eyes and holes; *cutting*, with chisels or sets, has already been touched on; and *welding*. Fire welding is a very different thing from the kind mentioned above, and calls for careful judgement of the heat of the metal, speed and deftness in hammering the pieces together, and a clean fire. It is not quickly mastered and it is one of the features by which good workmanship is to be judged. In all these operations the smith must know how to *take a heat* for his metal that is right for the job, ranging from a *warm heat*, that is just too hot to be touched with the hand, to *white* or *snowball heat*, by way of *black, blood, bright red, bright yellow, sweating* and *full welding heat*. Each is right for a different kind of work and recognising it takes some practice; and that is why the hearth is always situated in a gloomy corner of the shop, or at least where no sunlight can fall on it and disguise the colour of the metal.

Times change, methods change. The horse has given place to the car, the sickle to the combine harvester, wrought iron to mild steel. Blacksmiths no longer *fire the anvil* with black powder at weddings and jubilations, and on 23 November they go home to watch television rather than gathering to celebrate the feast of their patron, 'Old Clem' (St Clement), as they were still doing in parts of Hampshire into this century. But despite all, the blacksmith's forge remains to a remarkable degree what it always has been – the place where others are enabled to maintain their work, and at the same time a kind of social centre. Through the day, people drop in to bring, collect, or ask about jobs; the telephone interrupts with more enquiries; a couple of builder's men, clutching a rough pencil sketch of some fitting, wait for attention and pass the time with local gossip; and an old man who has known the forge since he was a boy, shuffles in for a warm and a chat (not too easy as he's stone deaf). Mr Pibworth receives them all with even good temper and continues to sort out bits of metal, draw diagrams, quote prices, sell lengths of steel, nuts, bolts and washers, give instructions, exchange news and get on with his cutting and welding. It is a scene of steady activity for the larger part of the day, with something timeless and undeniably satisfying about it.

# The boatbuilder

There is a centuries-old tradition of boatbuilding and shipbuilding along the shores and inlets of the Hampshire seaboard. Rural shipbuilding, it has been called, since in the days when timber was the chief material and more people lived in the countryside, it could be carried on away from large centres of population. It was when iron, then steel, ships started to be built that this kind of production began to give way in face of competition from the superior resources of new industrial areas, and the little slipways and their sawpits fell silent. During the last war, when all available capacity had to be brought into use, there was a certain revival of rural boatbuilding, and in recent years there has been a real boom with yards large and small catering for the weekend sailor.

Today, all ships are steel-built, while boats (that is, vessels with a displacement of less than about 100 tons) may be built of steel, aluminium alloy, glass fibre or wood, though the last is much less common than it used to be. There are pros and cons for each kind of boat. Steel is strong and completely watertight but prone to denting and rusting; aluminium alloy needs little maintenance but is subject to underwater electrolytic attack; glass fibre is easy to work and proof against most things, but may suffer deflection under load. Wood, the oldest material, is tough, resilient and can be worked to good lines, but is costly, in short supply and subject to rot and marine borers.

With one or two exceptions, boatbuilding is now so much a matter for industrialised production techniques that it is outside the scope of this survey. One of those exceptions is the wooden boat built largely on traditional lines. It still has plenty of admirers, especially among older sailors who look upon it as a 'living thing' with real personality. Ageing wooden boats can still command good prices, and whether old or new they have a prestige value that seems to increase with the preponderance of boats made of other materials.

One place where wooden boatbuilding is still carried on is Lymington,

B

33

the ferry terminal for the Isle of Wight, which stands on the western shore of the Solent. The real focus of this little town is not the attractive High Street but The Quay down to which it leads, where sailing enthusiasts gather or buy chandlery for their yachts moored at the huge marina in the Lymington River. Close by lies a boatyard where boats have been built since the 1820s, and here work is carried on that would be essentially recognisable to the craftsmen of five generations ago, though most of the tools and equipment are much altered and glass fibre hulls are to be seen alongside the wooden ones. It is, in fact, a place of evolving craftsmanship, where they make a traditional product by hand, using modern tools and techniques.

As the opportunities for practising hand skills become fewer those that remain are increasingly cherished. 'Thank God we're still making wooden boats,' is an expression of relief to be heard from men who have spent a lifetime in the work – men like Albert Doe for whom boats are their life and wood is a responsive material to be handled with understanding and appreciation. 'To me, wood is a living thing; glass fibre is cold, impersonal. Wood is everything.' A similar attitude is shared by the younger men too, and may help to explain the obvious interest of the apprentices in the work they are being trained to do.

Mr Doe began his five-year apprenticeship just before the Second World War broke out. During his first year his wages were 6/– (30p) a week, and out of that he was expected to begin buying his own tools! The boatbuilders still provide their own hand tools and a large assortment of padlocked tool chests is a feature of one of the buildings. Because boat-building was a reserved occupation, Mr Doe's busy war service was spent at the yard, where production was stepped up to build a 72 ft motor launch every month – so achieving a record ratio of output to labour. His training took him right through the mill, working in the mould loft, the rigging loft, the blacksmith's shop and the sawmill as well as in the building shed. Today's youngsters get much the same sort of experience, which makes for versatility and a strong team spirit that can overcome many production problems. Indeed, if any occupation could be called a team craft boatbuilding is the one, and in that respect it is unique among the crafts described in this book.

Every boat is conceived on the drawing board of its designer, who is known as a *naval architect*. He interprets the boat's structure in terms of buoyancy, water resistance, means of propulsion, accommodation and materials, keeping its ultimate use in mind all the time. As a blueprint for construction of the hull he makes a set of *lines drawings* which show the boat's lines from different viewpoints. The *Profile Plan* shows the boat from one side with the outline of *keel*, *sheer*, *stem* and *stern*. Below the keel

*A boat's lines are drawn up to full scale on the floor of the mould loft and any discrepancies corrected. Plywood moulds are made from the drawings as patterns for the main parts of the structure – in this case, the frames.*

is drawn an arbitrary baseline and above it a number of parallel *waterlines*, one of them, the *load waterline* or LWL, being the true waterline. Along the profile are drawn vertical *station lines*. The *Half Breadth Plan* shows one half of the hull from above. From this viewpoint, the waterlines appear as curves from end to end with the station lines at right-angles to the centre line. *The Body Plan* shows two views of the boat from dead ahead: on the right, from stem to midships, on the left, from midships to stern. Further lines, *diagonals* and *buttock lines* are drawn in to make additional reference points. *Tables of offsets* are provided with the lines drawings giving measurements to the various stations from baseline and centre line. Other plans drawn by the architect may include a *General Arrangement* of the boat – engine installation, sail plan, accommodation plan, deck plan and sundry detail drawings.

Working from drawings and offsets, the boat's lines are *laid off* to full scale on the floor of the *mould loft*, a wide gallery running the full 110 ft length of the building shed. The floor is painted white and the lines inked in using thin wooden battens to draw the curves; much of the drawing is done by the apprentices.By drawing the boat full size, details of construction can be accurately worked out and the boat's lines *made fair*, a phrase with variations, heard frequently and meaning that they follow accurate and pleasing curves. The table of offsets, it must be remembered, is made from quite small drawings, and when the latter are enlarged and faired out some discrepancies are inevitable.

To the layman, the mould loft drawings are about as comprehensible as an engineer's blueprint, but it helps to see the *moulds* being made from them. These are full-sized plywood patterns for the main structural members, sometimes also used to mark the positions of those members when the hull is building. Some of the moulds go to the sawmill for members which can be shaped from grown timber; others go to the laminating shed where complex curved members are built up. One of the causes contributing to the decline of wooden shipbuilding in the nineteenth century was a shortage of mature grown timber suitable for massive curved or angled pieces such as *knees* (brackets); only with the development of adequate glues in quite recent times has lamination become a practical proposition for large boats.

A slatted bench about 15 ft square is used for making up the laminations. The mould is laid on it and upright metal brackets are sited against both sides and bolted through the slats. The laminae, strips of freshly-glued timber, are placed on edge between the brackets and thus held in the desired curve until they have set; as they may be no more than $\frac{3}{8}$ in thick this is easily done. Thorough dryness is essential, ensured by stacking the timber for two or three days on the bench under a polythene cover with hot air blowing beneath. When matching curved members are wanted, a double-width lamination is made and cut down the middle; this is how the accurately-paired *frames* (ribs) of a boat are obtained. Some of the frames for lighter boats may be shaped by steaming lengths of American elm in a steam pipe, and then holding the curve firm until it sets. For most work on the hull, African iroko, in good supply and having little sapwood, is used.

One of the largest laminations commonly used is that for the *crook*, which joins stem to keel in a graceful curve. It may be as much as 20 ft long and composed of over fifty thicknesses of timber, and has to be shaped largely by hand. After the working profiles have been marked out, the larger areas of waste are removed with a power saw, but from this point on, adze, draw-knife, plane and chisel are used and the job may take all of three weeks to complete. The adze is one of the few traditional boatbuilding tools to remain in use and is capable of being used with surprising delicacy (though skill may be acquired at some cost: Mr Doe claims he has 'used an adze on most things and got scars to prove it'). Control is achieved

*The shipwright's adze, although of ancient origin, still has a useful place in today's tool kit. It is here being used in the shaping of a boat's crook, the huge lamination which joins stem and keel.*

by keeping one hand well up the shaft near the head and using the other for leverage. The boatbuilder's adze is recognisable by the projecting *peg-poll* behind the blade, formerly used for driving home deep any projecting nails when cleaning down the exterior of a large vessel.

The actual building of a large wooden boat must be among the most satisfying pieces of constructional work it is possible to see; and as it normally extends over several months, or even for a year, it is something that repays frequent visits. There is no denying that the shaping and fitting of timber on such a scale makes a compelling spectacle – as also does the diverse activity of the builders, working in groups or by themselves at the dozens of different operations involved in putting the curvaceous creature together. Fanciful though it may seem, one gets a curious impression that something with personality is being brought into being, a personality compounded of all the individual skills devoted to it; and that once down the slipway and in its true element it will come into a life of its own.

Laying a boat's keel usually means joining three or four substantial timbers and, in the case of sailing boats, incorporating a heavy lead or cast iron keel to give stability to the hull. At the fore end rises the stem, and at the after end the *sternpost*, which will support the *transom*. Accurate assembly of this backbone on the supporting *stocks* is vital to the subsequent structure and great pains are taken to ensure that it is done well.

When the frames are sited along both sides of the keel, the boat really begins growing and assumes a certain resemblance to the skeleton of a beached whale, while scaffolding rises round it to support narrow working plankways. To strengthen the union of frames and keel, a series of horizontal *floors* is bolted to both, together with numerous steel ties of which there may be sixty or seventy in a larger boat. These are specially made in the blacksmith's shop, as are all the numerous large bolts and special fittings. Stout wooden *stringers* run fore and aft inside the frames to strengthen them amidships.

Throughout the early stages of building, the frames are supported by a mass of strutting which is gradually removed as it becomes redundant. The edges of the erect frames onto which the planking will be laid are bevelled off to follow the line of the hull. Temporary *ribbands* go round the hull at vertical intervals of about 9 in so that its contours can be checked and made to come fair, an operation in which the builder's eye plays the major part. The upper ends of the frames are joined fore and aft by a *shelf* which also serves to support the deck beams running across the boat; siting of these beams is determined less by the frames than by the major features of the deck, such as skylights and masts.

There are several methods of planking hulls. In small *clinker-built* boats the planks are overlapped; in *carvel-built* boats they are butted together, running fore and aft in both cases. Large hulls may be double planked, with two diagonal skins at 90° to each other; or the planking may be diagonal inside, fore and aft outside. Double planking has great strength, even though the thickness of each skin may be as little as $\frac{1}{2}$ in or $\frac{5}{8}$ in. The planking is snugly rebated into the keel, stem and transom.

In the case of double planking, the first skin is fastened lightly and covered with calico sheeting which is painted with linseed oil. As the second skin goes on, the whole thickness is fastened very securely, making *ties* wherever a frame is covered and at each corner where the planks cross. Square-section copper *clenches* are used, passed through deeply countersunk drillings; two men work together to fasten them, one turning the end over a *roove* (washer) with a *dressing punch* and hammer, while the other steadies it from outside with a heavy steel *dolly* which has a *spicket* fitting the countersinking. There may be as many as 5000 clenches in a 50 ft boat and every one is put in by this laborious method. Afterwards, every countersinking is plugged with a glued *grain pin* cut across the grain with a circular cutter.

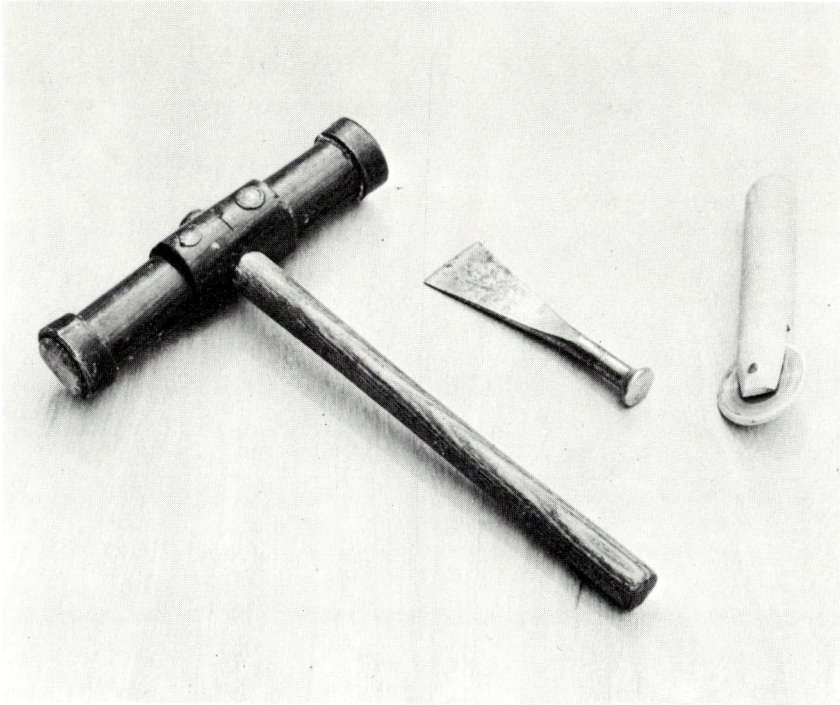

*A boat's seams must be made watertight by packing or caulking them with cotton or oakum. The caulking mallet and iron are the traditional tools for the job, while the wheel is a more recent device for caulking deck planking.*

Then the whole of the hull – no inconsiderable area – is *jacked off*, worked over with jack planes to fair out any unevennesses which may have come about in the course of planking. After this all seams are *caulked* to make them watertight, using heavy cotton above the waterline and oakum below. Two old tools are used for this job, a *caulking iron*, like a splayed chisel with a blunt edge, and a *caulking mallet* to drive it with. This is a curious tool, having a double head, copper-bound and slotted for most of its length. Just why it is preferable to a plain mallet no-one seems certain, though boatbuilders claim it gives a telling ring in use and is not tiring to handle. The caulked seams are further packed with thin glued wooden *splines* before the hull is cleaned down with wooden smoothing planes; use polishes their soles and makes them easy to work. After a final smooth-over with sanding machines the hull is painted; below the waterline it may be covered with nylon sheathing, a method of discouraging the Teredo worm for which the boatbuilders of old would have given their right arms.

Decks used to be made of substantial timber, but this has generally given way to plywood coated with nylon or glass fibre, or surfaced with thin teak planking. Caulking of deck seams is done with the aid of a small pressing wheel, following which the seams are filled with mastic applied from a nozzle. Varnished teak remains the most popular wood for rails and other exposed work above deck; it is one of the few traditional timbers still used on larger boats, along with Honduras and African mahogany, and Douglas fir for long straight members.

If the boat is to have an engine, whether as the chief means of propulsion or auxiliary to sails, it is usually installed by the marine fitters before any deck house is built and carefully levelled onto its prepared bed. Propeller shaft tubes are housed in *sterntube chocks* built onto the hull on either side of the keel and their correct alignment is critical to avoid all possibility of vibration.

One of the few separate trades in the boatyard is that of joiner, to whom falls the responsibility for interior fitting work such as cabins, cupboards and companion ways. With his work, the boat starts to take on a finished appearance below deck. Compared with the hull this is light woodwork but in a small craft it can make a useful contribution to the boat's strength. At this stage there is till plenty to do above deck and there may be spars, rigging, winches, davits, rails, glazing and many other features to be fitted. Outside contractors are usually brought in to install navigational equipment and do the electrical work which is often extensive. The more luxurious kind of boat may have air conditioning, hot showers, television, a washing machine and a galley that would do justice to a modern apartment.

There will probably be a certain amount of fitting still to be done when the boat is finally launched. That is one of the special days in the yard's routine, and calls not only for the exercise of necessary skill but also for proper observance. It is commonly held that to be successful in competitive sailing a boat should never be launched 'dry' and never on a Friday – certainly not on a Friday the thirteenth. 'If anything's going to go wrong', Mr Doe warns, 'it'll go wrong on that day!'

So a boat takes shape, through months of planning and building, with the exercise of many skills and much traditional wisdom. It is a major feat of craftsmanship and a thing of great beauty. The men who make the boats are plain men, not much given to eulogising their work, but Albert Doe has an estimate of it that probably speaks for all of them when he says: 'It's not a trade, it's a creation really.'

# The stonemason

Most of us have to admit, if we are honest, that we take very little notice of the stonemason's handiwork, and ironically this is often the case in old towns, where it has become part of a familiar landscape: on a large scale in churches, monuments and public buildings, and on a smaller one in many details of construction. Yet all of them bear witness to the mason's skill in handling a material which for centuries was held to be the proper one for all important buildings and the houses of the wealthy. It was not until quite recent times that steel and concrete were accepted as adequate alternatives to traditional building materials, in response to the demand for speedier erection of bigger buildings by less labour-intensive methods. Now, the only occasions when stonemasonry gets more than a cursory glance may be when we gaze with awe at some cathedral or stately home – or are faced with the problem of choosing a suitable headstone. That is when the cost of craftsmanship comes home with a shock, as it is explained how the stone has to be quarried, transported, sawn, trimmed, lettered and polished before being placed on site, each stage involving a great deal of hand work.

So, while a noble past may justly be claimed for the mason's craft, its future cannot but seem clouded. Modern constructional methods have made the use of stone a rarity in most parts of the country except for prestige buildings, and today's curious economics of supply can sometimes mean that artificial stone is more readily obtainable than real, even in a natural stone region. In fact, to keep his head above water, the mason has to rely heavily upon fireplace and monumental work and even the latter has been reduced in recent years by the trend towards fewer and neater churchyard memorials. Nevertheless, the skills of those who work in stone are sure to survive, for this challenging natural material will always be in demand where a combination of durability and beauty is wanted, and, as will be seen, there is another special reason why we should continue to value the work of the mason.

Harry Blackwell, who runs a family firm in Winchester, is well aware of the problems, for he has seen business fall off drastically since he was apprenticed before the war; then, the firm employed eighteen men – now, it is down to a third of that number. He is, not without reason, pessimistic about the trade, sensing that stone is no longer held to be of importance to the community, and feeling it all the more poignantly as a fourth-generation craftsman. His great-grandfather worked on the Menai Bridge and his grandfather came to Hampshire working on railway construction, becoming foreman, and later owner, of a firm of Winchester stonemasons. It was probably his grandfather's influence that led Mr Blackwell to follow the same calling, for after his father's early death, he spent a lot of time in the mason's yard with him, listening to talk of stone and the men who built the great castles and churches of the Middle Ages. So he joined the firm and went through the mill as an apprentice; for his first month he got no pay, but after that things improved to half a crown a week.

There is a tendency for stonemasons to specialise in different kinds of work, depending on the stone occurring in their area. Thus, a Scottish firm may concentrate on granite work calling for the use of heavy tools suited to such intractable rock, another may work chiefly with one of the soft Cotswold limestones, or may specialise in decorative marble work. Mr Blackwell is a general mason using mostly Purbeck, Swanage and Portland stones – which do not have to travel too far – and carrying out all kinds of construction and repairs; he may be asked to make things as various as fireplaces and garden seats and headstones. There is a steady demand for headstones, which makes it worthwhile for one of his men to specialise in letter cutting; Mr Blackwell points out that an attractive memorial can be either complemented or spoiled by the quality of its lettering.

The firm does, however, have a field in which they have developed a special interest over the last half-century – the repair of ancient buildings. This is work which calls for a degree of understanding perhaps a little out of the ordinary, and for the establishment of good working relationships with those architects who specialise in building restoration. There are times when it can mean taking on jobs fifty or sixty miles from home, but much of the firm's activity is no more than a stone's throw away, at Winchester College and the Cathedral of St Swithun. Here are two groups of buildings that stand as splendid examples of the mason's skill in times past, both of them providing an alarming demonstration of the ravages of weather and atmospheric pollution. On these two establishments alone, Mr Blackwell and his men have spent nearly three-quarters of their labours for many years, and it is to their skill, under the enlightened direction of the responsible authorities, that so much of the clean, well-kept appearance of the buildings is due.

Under ideal conditions, worked stone acquires a hardened 'skin' that is its best protection, but town buildings have for centuries been subject to an insidious assault from the sulphuric impurities in the atmosphere, contributed by industry and the domestic coal fire. They dissolve in rain to form a weak sulphuric acid which reacts to limestone surfaces, forming a crust with soot and dirt; such surfaces may appear quite sound until the crust is damaged, whereupon it begins to peel off and expose the soft interior to the weather. Water, too, absorbed by porous stone, may freeze in winter and expand to cause cracks and flaking. An expedition round the parapets and catwalks of the Cathedral roof shows how extensive this problem is, while the very size of the building suggests that it will require attention from the masons far into the forseeable future.

In addition to actual repair work, a regular programme of cleaning is desirable, for this both improves the appearance of stonework and removes dangerous pollutants. Hoses are fixed to direct a steady spray onto the masonry, which is then brushed down with scrubbing brushes when the dirt has loosened – as little as two hours may be enough. Repairs, on the other hand, may mean anything from cutting out and replacing odd stones that have suffered badly, to the replacement of an entire window. The renewal of a much-corroded flying buttress and its associated pinnacle on the northeast corner of the retrochoir, was a good opportunity to follow the course of one such operation (it took several weeks) and to see many of the tools and methods described below in use.

The first necessity in a restoration job like this is to draw up on squared paper an exact plan, and elevations showing the position of every stone, as each one will be copied and damaged sections of carving reconstructed. We can see straight away that some familiarity with details of historic ornament as well as with building methods is called for if this is to be done properly.

Ketton stone from Rutland has been specified for use in Winchester Cathedral repairs for many years because it has a granular structure, somewhat like fish-roe, that tends to shed water. It is delivered by rail and lorry to the workshop where it has first to be cut up into manageable pieces. Primary cuts are made with a large suspended frame saw, electrically powered, that can incorporate a tungsten-tipped blade for soft stones or a mild steel blade, fed with grit or carborundum granules, for hard ones. A circular saw with a 4 ft 6 in blade deals with stone up to 18 in thick, while smaller pieces of dry, soft stone are cut up in the workshop with hand saws. However it is done, carefully-planned sawing is economical of stone and saves much cutting away of surplus.

Inside the workshop, the masons work at a row of stone benches or *bankers*, large blocks of stone about 3 ft high on which the workpieces rest,

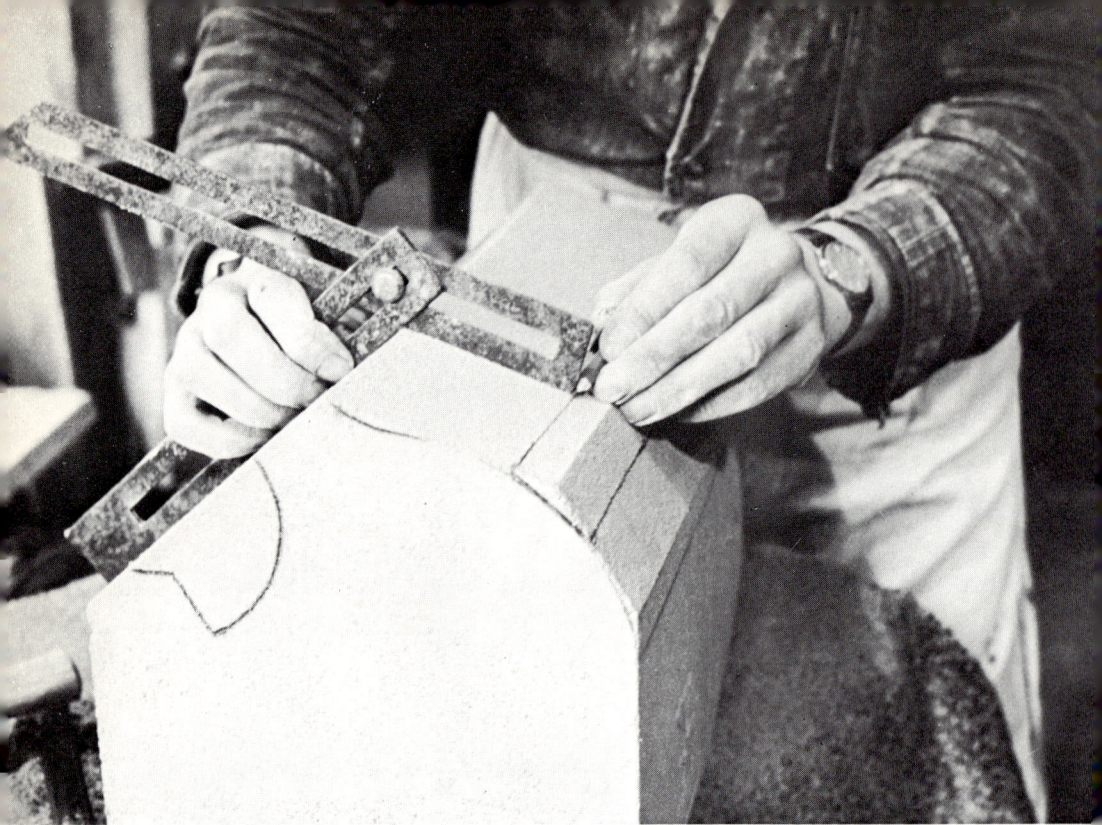

*When making a moulding (as here, for a window) the mason first outlines the profile with a template, then uses an adjustable bevel to mark off the salient features before removing waste stone. Thus the profile is correctly maintained, even along curved mouldings.*

cushioned on old blankets or pieces of carpet. In large firms, those who work indoors are known as *banker hands* and those who go out on site as *fixing masons*. The mason's chief cutting tools are chisels, and they fall into two categories: those with small striking ends for use with the hammer, and those with wide striking ends that will not damage a wooden mallet. Included in the first group, and mostly used in the early stages of reducing blocks of stone, are the *punch* with a very small blade and the *pitching tool* with a wide one. They are used with a short-handled hammer.

The first step in dressing a stone to the required dimensions is to produce a *master face*, working from the edges inwards, first with a rather narrow chisel and then with a broad-bladed *boaster*. This is used with a conical beechwood mallet of some 6-8 in diameter. On particularly hard stone a *claw boaster* with a coarsely-toothed edge is used. When the surface is level, it is sighted against two straight edges to ensure that it has been *taken out of twist*. With the master surface made, the other faces of the stone can be accurately cut and checked with the aid of set-square or bevel. The stonemason takes pains to ensure that as each building unit is shaped

*A mason's mark identifies both his work and his tools. Besides the hammer, these are a point, two boasters ( with wide mallet ends) and a claw boaster.*

from irregular raw material it will fit perfectly into the completed whole.

When a stone is to be worked for a moulding it is first cut to the overall dimension of the section, which is drawn on the ends with a zinc template. An adjustable bevel is set as a guide for a pencil and the longitudinal lines of the moulding drawn. With chisel or boaster the mason removes surplus stone along the planes indicated and so ensures that the correct section is maintained until the moulding has been fully developed. Wooden-handled gouges are used to cut concave mouldings and a negative template used to check their depth; a further template is made if the moulding follows a curve. Like any other material, stone is liable to present unexpected faults and problems; sometimes a hard filling is found in a natural cavity and this *snotty piece*, as it is called, must be worked carefully.

Surface finishing of the stone can be carried out in many ways. Where a plain surface is wanted, the face of the stone is worked over with a hand-held *drag*, a steel scraper with a saw edge; variously-shaped ones are used to finish mouldings. To give a really smooth finish, the stone can be rubbed over with sand and water with a piece of harder stone. Then there is a

45

range of finishes which can be used to achieve effects of texture; for example, *pointing* and *hammer dressing*, which produce a very fine or a coarse, irregular surface respectively. Two finishes used a lot in Mr Blackwell's workshop are *tooling*, continuous parallel lines made with the boaster, and *droving*, short parallel lines made in regular rows. Very hard and fine-grained stones can be polished with beeswax.

Each surface of the stone which is to be mortared to others is lightly pecked over to encourage adhesion, and a code letter and number are cut on every stone to show its position in the structure. A further mark – the *mason's mark* – shows who was responsible for dressing it; it may be a monogram or some simple device which is personal to each mason and it also goes on all his tools.

When cutting of the stones is nearing completion, it is time to start dismantling the old masonry. Scaffolding is erected by contractors to Mr Blackwell's requirements and a hut for the use of his men is put up on a corner of the roof. This is not really the luxury it might seem, for tools have to be kept somewhere and it is a long way down to the ground; moreover, the higher parts of a cathedral are very exposed to wind and weather and working up there on a cold March day can be uncomfortably like lingering on the north face of Snowdon. Before the old buttress is taken down, a strong wooden framework is made to fit snugly under it; this allows the worn stones to be lifted off one by one and the new ones later to rest at the correct curvature while the mortar sets.

A mason has to be adept at handling heavy stone. On the ground, pieces of many tons' weight can be raised several feet by the use of crow-bars and blocks, but the infinitely easier electric hoist is used to get new stones up to the Cathedral roof. Once there, they are moved on a small trolley to the scaffolding and then hauled up by a pulley and *lewis*, one of the mason's most useful pieces of equipment. It takes various forms, but the principle of all is the same: the gripping power of a wedge inverted in the stone. A hole 6 in deep is cut in the top surface, widened towards its base. Into this drops the lewis, which may be a split bolt with the upper ends curved and eyed and a ring passing through the eyes. The two parts of the bolt face away from each other and when the ring is lifted it applies leverage, forcing the lower ends outwards against the stone. Three or four tons can be hoisted in this simple way.

Each stone is carefully placed in its predetermined position and mortared to its neighbours, though it is accuracy of cutting and fit as much as any mortar which holds masonry soundly together. The mortar gap between the stones is approximately $\frac{1}{8}$ in, checked by the insertion of four small pieces of slate or hardboard; pieces of oyster shell were used in the Middle Ages and come to light when old masonry is being taken down. As the

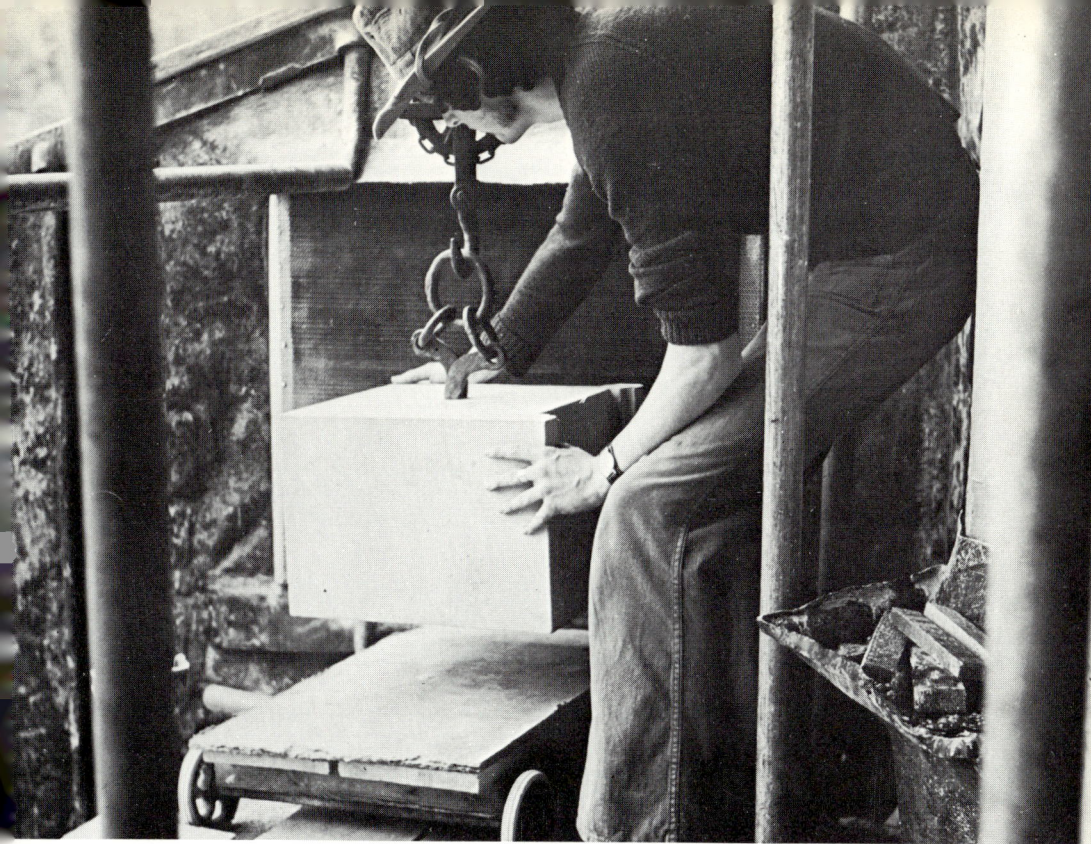

*Large blocks of stone can easily be raised with a lewis, which employs the principle of an inverted wedge in a hole. In this instance outward thrust on a split bolt is imparted by the lifting rings.*

fresh, new stonework is assembled, it looks impressively crisp and correct against the time-worn backdrop of the ancient building; an effect which has only been achieved by the weeks of meticulous measuring and shaping which have gone before. Stonemasons have always set great store by accuracy and good workmanship and one can see why their equipment was adopted to symbolise the beliefs of freemasonry.

When the mortar has hardened, the finishing touch is given: the buttress is worked over with a drag to tidy up any slight irregularity or misplacement of the stones that might have caused a lip. After all, when a man knows his work will probably remain standing for the scrutiny of some fellow-craftsman in five centuries' time, he wants to make sure it's presentable.

# The tailor

Few craftsmen have quite such a close relationship with their customers as the tailor. 'You are always extending the personality of the client who has his clothes made by you. You're not just wrapping round so many yards or inches of cloth in the semblance of a garment: you are always trying to express what the man wants to look like and what he wants to be like.' So asserts Henry Thornton, tailor and breeches maker, whose premises are situated not far from the bustle of the High Street in Winchester. It is a relationship that may begin as soon as a customer steps into the shop and continue for years, through many suits and even the re-cutting of a suit made for the man's father thirty years back. There are creative possibilities in his work which Mr Thornton finds especially appealing and there are doubtless more than a few men in business and public life who owe him credit for his ability to create the image of success.

For over a century, tailoring has been the subject of increasingly successful attempts at mass-production, beginning with the widespread adoption of the sewing machine in the 1860s. Today, most clothes are factory-made and a suit from a ready-made store is within the range of most pockets; why then, one may ask, does the bespoke tailor still thrive? The answer lies in the difference between salesmanship and craftsmanship, with all that the latter implies of hand skill and individuality. The salesman has only to fit his customers to his range of fittings and styles, but the tailor must rise to the challenge of actually making garments which will fit and enhance the figure before him. And in these days the enjoyment of personal attention may well be a luxury more desirable than ever before.

Tailors have been studying the geometry of the human form for a long time in their quest for the elusive perfect fit. What is believed to be the earliest extant book on the subject was written by a Spaniard, Juan de Alcega, in 1589 and it was followed in due course by many others. But despite plenty of ingenious calculations, the art of *cutting* remained for most small tailors a somewhat hit-and-miss affair until about the end of the last century. In evidence of this there survives an appealing story of a German tailor's wife who is said to have put her children to bed with the words: 'My dears! Now pray for your father, for he has a coat to cut.' Today, most suits are cut according to what is known (coincidentally) as the Thornton system, but since a surprising number of us have some oddity of build there can be no final substitute for the tailor's experienced eye. As Mr Thornton says, 'One is thinking all the time of style, rather than slavish adherence to a system.'

An atmosphere of dignified calm pervades Mr Thornton's shop. The corner showroom has large windows whose lower halves are discreetly backed with the fine-mesh wire screens which used to be the sign of good-class tailors' shops; they allow one to see out rather than in, and in the old days were used to display the arms of local families who patronised the business. Inside, on a large table and a carved sideboard, lies a range of manufacturers' sample books, containing some six or seven thousand cloths. Shelves on one wall hold a number of lengths of suiting. There are a couple of chairs and some magazines.

The first decisions about the customer's requirements are made here in the showroom where the tailor is able to draw on his huge range of styles and cloths – everything from a 6 oz worsted for the businessman going to the tropics to a 21 oz tweed for the shooting man going to the moors (the weights are for a yard of 60 in width). In the showroom, too, the tailor begins to assess the customer's personality, to guide him gently if his choice of pattern or style seems unsuitable and to observe any disadvantages of figure or deportment. To leave this until the *fitting room* may well be too late, for as one of the craft pointed out a long time ago, 'It is very necessary to observe well a man before measuring him, so as to note his ordinary posture, and that without warning him, for he may stoop naturally, or hold himself erect, or else lean on one side or the other; if he expects that you are going to take his measure, he will think he is doing right to hold himself more erect than normal and you will fail with your measure.'

Height, chest and seat are the three basic *measures* from which the tailor works, though Mr Thornton normally takes twenty-three all told and would take another seven in the case of a customer not likely to be readily available if ordering riding breeches later. In earlier times, measures used to be recorded in the form of strips of brown paper or parchment.

A start is made on cutting the pattern as soon as possible, preferably within half a day, while the customer's characteristics are still fresh in Mr Thornton's mind. He will probably call on his *gods* to help him in this – a collection of standard patterns on thick paper which are used as a guide to basic outlines to save repetitious work. The pattern is drawn

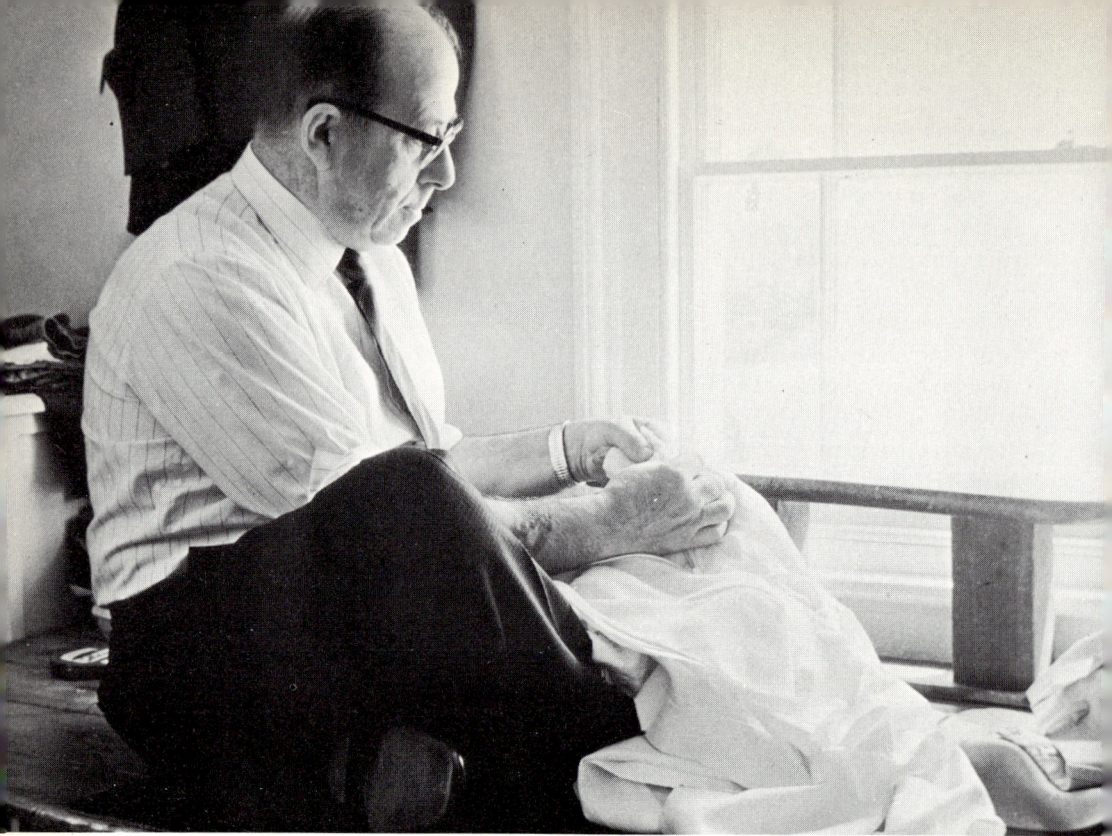

*Few tailors sit cross-legged at their work these days, but this demonstration shows how the posture allows a knee to be used as a sewing support.*

with the aid of a *graduated scale*, which gives a guide to the proportions of any size, and a *square*, a right-angled rule which does the same in respect of the details of coats. A *trouser cutter's curve*, whose two edges follow different curves like a scimitar blade, gives the line for inside and outside leg seams. Plain measuring is done with a *yardstick*, so called whether 36 in or 48 in long. The pattern is cut from brown kraft paper with hollow-ground *pattern shears* and is transferred to the cloth by drawing round with *tailor's chalk*, which is a small pipeclay square with knife-like edges. When for any reason it is necessary to transfer a chalk line from the cloth to the pattern, a *tracing wheel* pricks right through to the paper; it is handy, for example, when making an experimental alteration during fitting.

The leading figure in operations so far is the *cutter*, who is the kingpin of any tailoring business whether or not he is the owner. It is he who meets and influences the customer, exercises his practised eye in the niceties of style and fit and sets the standard of workmanship for the rest of the staff. His particular domain is the *cutting room*, where he is under-studied by the *assistant cutter* or *striker* whose basic job is to put the patterns on the cloth and generally assist. It is held to be an excellent way of learning a trade

50

in which experience born of continual practice counts for much more than any theoretical training.

Each piece of a pattern is marked with the customer's name and a sample of the cloth is attached to one of them; others will be added if he orders more suits later and so a kind of dossier is built up. By folding the pattern pieces in half and making two V cuts, they are given diamond-shaped holes through which tape is looped to hang them up.

When it comes to cutting out the cloth, the cutter's most valued piece of equipment comes into use – his heavy *cutting shears* which he alone handles. Weighing, as Mr Thornton's do, 3¼ lb, they cannot be wielded like scissors and must be used on the bench or *cutting board* – they are made with resting surfaces. To use them requires a muscular effort from the shoulder which can be tiring even to the experienced if there are three or four suits to be cut. Most cloths are folded for cutting and afterwards the salient features are outlined by sewing through the two thicknesses with white cotton; when the cotton is cut to separate the pieces, each is identically marked. Linings and canvasses (the hidden panels that give a coat substance and shape), are cut out with a light pair of *narrow shears*.

The pieces of a garment all being ready, they are folded into a neat bundle, tied with tape and sent with a garment ticket to the *workroom*. The parcel for a coat will contain cloth, lining, facing, canvas, buttons and button silk. At this point, the cutter must decide which of his workpeople is to do the making up, for there is considerable specialisation in the trade and even in small firms one man may be good with a certain kind of garment, another with a certain style of work. Several of Mr Thornton's staff are outworkers, typifying today's independence and the liking of women, particularly, for work which will fit in with domestic commitments.

Making up a suit is done in three stages. The first is the production of a *pocket baiste*, in which the body seams are sewn, the *foreparts* joined and the canvasses, pockets, sleeves and collar are tacked in. About a morning's work is needed but it can be reduced to something like an hour and a half by simplifying the sewing to make a *flash baiste*, which is sometimes necessary when speed is called for or an elaborate check has to be tried on for accuracy of fit. This brings the suit to the *first fitting*.

If extensive corrections are called for, the suit may be taken apart and re-cut as required; the pattern will also be adjusted. The suit now goes to the *forward baiste* stage in which the edges, facings and pockets are permanently made up and the collar partly made. The collar and lapels are lined with canvas and melton cloth and worked over with a *padding stitch* to induce them to lie with a slight curve to the body. The suit is now ready for the *second fitting*, when any further corrections are made.

In the *finishing stage* the side, shoulder and sleeve seams are permanently

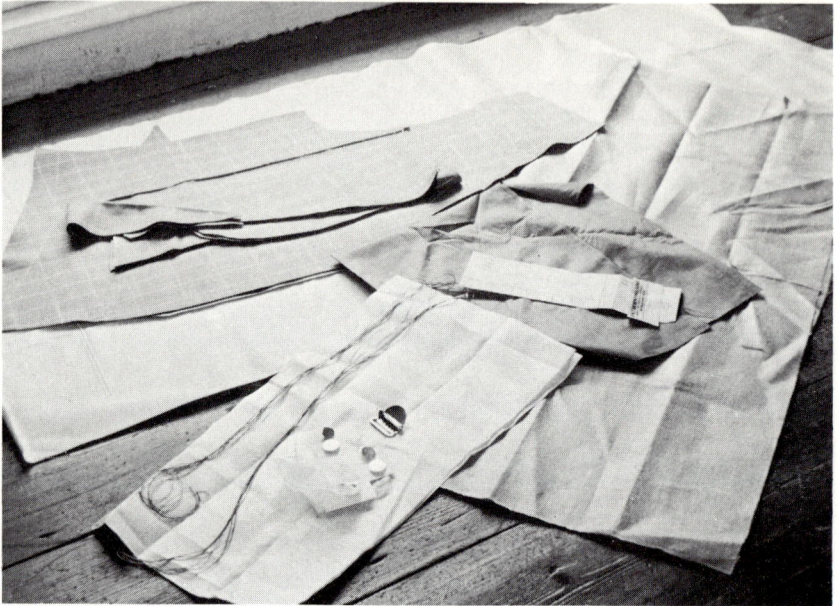

*The materials for a waistcoat sent in a bundle to the workroom by the cutter. They comprise cloth, lining, facing, canvas, buttons, adjuster, button silk and garment ticket.*

sewn and the collar finished, button holes are made and the edge stitching done. Then the suit is pressed and the buttons attached ready for the final *third fitting*.

Throughout the making of a suit, the iron is in frequent use and one can offer no better appraisal of its importance to the tailor than that from Mr Thornton's own lips: 'The iron plays an enormous part in bespoke tailoring. The iron shapes the canvasses; the iron shapes the cloth; the iron shapes the seams; no seam fits a body without it being pressed in a prescribed way to fit that seam to the body. And then, when the final finishing comes it is only a smoothing process because all the shape has gone into the garment.' It is not, therefore, in any boastful sense that he adds, 'With an iron, I can make a good garment even better.'

Pressing itself has become a specialisation among London outworkers and some elaborate irons are used. But the important thing is that the iron should be weighty. In Mr Thornton's workroom electric irons are used mostly, but for certain jobs he still keeps a set of old *goose irons* with their gas heating stand. They are of cast iron, ranging from 6–26 lb weight and are useful where a cooling heat is wanted; the heaviest are used on really weighty cloths, such as livery cloths of 30 oz or more. The curious name

*There is a certain appeal in the survival of old practices; in this tailor's workroom a horseshoe continues in use as a rest for hot electric irons.*

for this iron probably derives from the open-ended handle which gives it the appearance of a bird on the water, and it is said that new ones were supplied coated with goose-grease; Mr Thornton certainly has pungent memories of new irons being heated for the first time. Although the older irons are not much used these days, it is interesting to see the traditional iron rest still in use in the workroom – an old horseshoe nailed to a square piece of wood. Goose irons, of course, could always be dropped in a bucket of water to cool them if they got too hot, an advantage definitely not shared by electric ones! When the soles became pitted they were rubbed with soap on a linen pad as a filler. Various boards and pads are used as ironing accessories, delightfully distinguished by such names as *donkey* (double sleeve board), *baby* and *dolly*.

The tailor's equipment is for the most part quite simple and the only large items in Mr Thornton's workroom are electric and treadle sewing machines. The electric ones have limited use, chiefly for long straight seams; treadles run slower and are easier to control. It is the humble needle that still does most of the work. Needles come in three kinds: *sharps* which are long and thin, *betweens* which are rather thicker, and *ground-downs* which are very thick. Since it is not worth his while to retrieve them when dropped, a tailor gets through a great many. His *thimble* is topless, pushed with the back of the third finger. An aptitude for sewing is an important qualification for a youngster making a beginning in the trade. The aim is to develop an action so smooth that there is no discernible pause between one stitch and the next, the needle being pushed with the third finger while held between the thumb and first, and picked up by the two latter as it comes through the cloth. Quality of workmanship is judged, as with saddlers and sailmakers, largely by the sewing.

Tailoring, it is pleasing to discover, preserves a rich private vocabulary that the customer is unlikely to be aware of. The cutter is known to the staff as *his nibs*, the assistant cutter as *umsies*. Surplus cuttings are *mungo*, and are a traditional perk for both cutting room and workroom staff, though not readily saleable now because of their synthetic content. A person difficult to get on with is likened to a cloth difficult to handle, hence a *soft sew*. Repairing and altering is *codging*, bad work is *skimping*, *dead* work has been paid for in advance and still has to be done. Falling behind is known as being *in the drag* and may mean asking someone to *give a piece out*, a helping hand, also appreciated when a job is wanted in a hurry, a *skiffle*. When a suit is refused by a customer or suffers some kind of cutting disaster it becomes *pork* – is this perhaps an expression of anathema deriving from the Jewish background of many tailoring businesses? If a workman has presumed too far upon the affections of his young lady and they have *baisted up a small job* she is *in canvas* and it is to be hoped he will marry her and make her his *hipstay;* he may also have to ask his employer for an advance of pay, *the boot*.

There has always been a strong freemasonry in the craft, and Mr Thornton relates one example which was probably being practised as late as the 1930s. A journeyman (itinerant) tailor in difficulties would go into any tailor's shop and draw a chalk circle on the counter; it indicated without need of words that he was in financial straits and a whip-round would produce some small change in the circle to help him on his way.

Among the unusual garments that Mr Thornton turns out are some which are an inseparable part of the Winchester scene; they are the gowns worn by Scholars of Winchester College, and those worn by the elderly residents of the twelfth-century Hospital of St Cross, mulberry-coloured for the Brethren of Noble Poverty and black for Bishop Blois' foundation. He has been called on to make outfits for a modern coaching enthusiast; the driver's coat of 34 oz boxcloth was surely substantial enough to keep out the very worst of weather.

Tailoring was in his family blood but Mr Thornton went into it the more readily as a youngster because he saw it offered certain opportunities for travel – a small number of West End firms have always sent staff abroad for important clients – and in the course of time such opportunities did come his way. During the war he served with the RAF and spent five long years kitting out recruits, sometimes a thousand in a day. Afterwards he went back with relief to tailoring of the more creative kind and eventually started his own business. Now it is a family affair in which his wife and one of his sons share, the latter making the fourth generation of Thorntons to have followed the same calling.

# The thatcher

There seems to be something emotive about thatching. The sight of a thatcher at work on a roof with his ladder planted in the highway, or of some newly-thatched cottage, is enough to give many people a glow of satisfaction at the survival of an ancient craft and a conviction that the countryside must be in good heart. Truly, well-maintained thatch *is* one of the visual delights of the countryside. But it is more than just a picturesque survival from another age; it is an entirely practical roofing material that is, moreover, an excellent use of natural resources readily available in many places.

The thatcher himself – doubtless because his handiwork is more apparent than most – is often held up as the typical traditional craftsman and hence a vanishing species; but it is good to be able to report otherwise, for such is the stimulus created by well-to-do settlers in the countryside renovating their cottages, that thatching is booming as never before. And for this conservation of our heritage of rural architecture we should be thankful. A glance at the yellow pages of the telephone directory in many southern areas will confirm that the craft is far from being on its last legs.

A man whose work is well known on the eastern side of Hampshire is George Barrett of Bentworth, who in some ways represents the modern kind of thatcher. Unlike the older generation who worked in a limited area he is mobile and thinks nothing of travelling thirty miles to a job; this reflects both the smaller number of thatchers about today and the decreasing number of roofs that remain thatched, for many have been changed in favour of slates or tiles and thatched ricks are a thing of the past. Then, instead of working alone or with just the assistance of a son, as often used to be the case, he employs a team that is four strong at times – one son included. Master thatchers used to dislike taking on more than one assistant in order to save work for their sons, but as sons are not under the same pressure these days to follow their fathers, there is room for newcomers. Mr Barrett is also typical of the newer thatchers in practising all three main kinds of thatching, a versatility promoted, as will be seen, by the difficulties of modern times.

Those who have never given thatched roofs more than a passing glance may be forgiven for assuming that one is very much like another. Yet not only are three different techniques employed but there are various ways in which the thatcher may show his individuality and skill. The first of these techniques is *long-straw*, characteristic of corn-growing regions. Threshed wheat straw is laid and combed out to produce a distinctive flowing appearance which is easily recognised; it is secured at ridge and eaves by split hazel *spars*, often arranged in a diamond pattern. Long-straw alone is secured at the eaves.

The second technique is *Norfolk reed*, universally regarded as best of all in terms of durability and appearance. Reed from regularly-harvested beds is laid butt end down and dressed to produce a neat, close-cropped effect, like a series of quills, from which rain is rapidly shed. Eaves and gables are shaped by beating the butts into position. Norfolk reed is too stiff to bend for the ridge and another marsh plant, sedge, is generally used, held down by a pattern of spars.

The third technique is *combed wheat reed*, also known as *reed straw* and *Devon reed*. Although wheat straw is the material used, the method is so similar to Norfolk reed that it is helpful to consider them together. Prepared straw is laid butt downwards and dressed to the roofline like Norfolk reed but it is ridged with straw rather than sedge, while eaves and gables are trimmed by cutting to make edges somewhat sharper than Norfolk reed. Practice is needed to distinguish the two kinds. It is doubtful if a Devonshire origin can actually be claimed for combed wheat reed but it is certainly common in Devon and Dorset and is also often used elsewhere.

Modern farming practice has had considerable effect on thatching in the last thirty years, the chief agent of change being the combine harvester. Indeed, the influence of this juggernaut on many aspects of country life makes an interesting study. For the combine to operate most effectively, short-stemmed wheat is preferred and leaves least straw to be disposed of -- and that too crushed to be of use. Hence, varieties have been bred to suit the machine and the thatcher has had great difficulty in getting long-stemmed straw, with the result that Norfolk reed has become popular in the traditional long-straw areas. However, George Barrett and others have made efforts to persuade farmers to grow taller varieties and it looks as if the situation has been saved. Supplies now seem to be much better than they have been for a long time and some farmers are actually finding it more profitable to grow wheat for straw than for grain.

Thatching, like many another craft, follows no standard procedure and varies considerably from area to area and even from thatcher to thatcher. The following account can therefore do no more than indicate what one might expect to find going on in the Hampshire area, making reference to Mr Barrett's methods and terms as they occur.

Wheat for long-straw work must be handled with care to avoid crushing and should be fed through the threshing machine so that it comes out with the stalks lying parallel. When the thatcher receives it he starts work by making a *bed*, shaking out the straw with a pitchfork in layers but keeping the stalks lying together as much as possible; it is then liberally watered and left for an hour or two to reach the right condition for laying. After that, the tedious business of *yealming* can begin. Walking backwards along the side of the bed, the thatcher draws out double handfuls of straw and gradually makes a long, tidy layer on the ground; then he moves forward, packing the straw against his feet to make tight bundles about 18 in deep by 4 in thick, cleaning out any short waste as he does so. These bundles are the *yealms*, the units of construction in long-straw work. Mr Barrett has found that it speeds up work to keep one member of his team busy on yealming back at the yard – the yealms are then taken in quantity to the site, ready for use.

Special oversize yealms are tied up to make the *eaves bundles* which form the first layer along eaves and gables, and over them go the yealms, each one overlapping the previous one by about two-thirds. There are various ways of attaching the yealms, the traditional method being to hold them under split hazel rods (*ledgers* or *sways*) tied or held by iron hooks to the rafters. Mr Barrett ties the eaves bundles and every fourth *course* of yealms with twine alone. Having thus secured the *undercoat*, the subsequent layers of the *top coat* are pegged in with *spars* which are concealed as work proceeds.

Spars are lengths of split, pointed hazel about 24-30 in long, twisted in the middle and bent double to form 'hairpins'; twisting prevents the outer fibres splitting and letting water into the grain. A great many are used in long-straw work, smaller quantities in reed work; Mr Barrett and his team get through about 2000 a week. Some thatchers make their own – a useful job for bad weather – but, as described in another chapter, there are still men here and there who specialise in spar making. Wherever possible, spars are pushed in at such an angle that they will not form channels for the entry of rainwater.

To carry yealms up to the roof a *yoke* is employed – a light, forked branch about 3 ft long into which the yealms are packed and secured by a strap or cord slipped over the branch ends. Up to ten of the heavy damp yealms can be lifted in this way and kept conveniently to hand on the roof. A thatcher, of course, spends much of his time up ladders and experience teaches him how far he can safely lean from them. In the days when ladder making was still a hand craft and thatchers often made their own from larch poles, they could be recognised by having the rounded sides innermost to be easier on the knees. Stout knee pads are still an essential item of thatching equipment.

In long-straw work, the thatcher works round the roof from right to left in vertical courses of about two ladder widths, keeping his weather eye open lest he should expose too much of the roof to possible storms if the old thatch is being completely stripped. As the yealms go on, he keeps them packed snugly together with spars stuck in the layer below to hold in the unfinished side temporarily. From time to time he goes over newly-completed areas with his *rake* to beat and comb out the straw and remove loose pieces. Rakes vary, but are usually about 2 ft long with teeth made of large nails spaced 2 in apart; sometimes one end is extended to form a handle.

When the apex of the roof is reached, a good watertight joint is required where the two sides meet. A roll of straw, known to Mr Barrett as a *dolly*, is tied along the ridge board and the topmost yealms are bent over and secured to it. A capping is generally made by bending extra long yealms over the ridge and holding them by the familiar pattern of ledgers known as *diamond work*. If a ridge with cut pattern is wanted, then the capping must be thicker so that the edges can be trimmed with a small *pattern knife* and a pair of sheep shears; Mr Barrett sometimes uses a trimming tool of his own devising, a pointing trowel with sharpened edges. Diamond work and patterns vary regionally and are also features through which the thatcher can express his individuality. The eaves and gables of long-straw work have to be secured against the wind by ledgers or diamond work and the roof corners are often held by single ledgers placed one above the other.

For all ridging Mr Barrett is increasingly using a technique that originates in the southwest. Long handfuls of straw are folded and twisted in the middle to form knuckles that are tied together in inverted V form; lengths are made up about 2-3 ft long and placed like ridge tiles to be held by the diamond work.

The kind of reed used for Norfolk reed thatching grows in many parts of Britain, but only in the marshy creeks of Norfolk is it regularly harvested on a large scale – and regularity is important since an annual cut is necessary to maintain proper quality of growth. Reed has the merit of needing little preparation on the thatcher's part, but the cutting is no light job, since it must wait until frost has removed the *flag* (leaves) and continue until the *colts* (new growth) begin to show: that is, through the coldest part of the winter. Until a few years ago, reed was cut by sickle or scythe and the number of men willing to undertake such wet and chilly work was

*How knuckles of straw are twisted, then tied with binder twine, to make up sections of ridge capping.*

decreasing; but the situation has been improved by the development of a mechanical cutter. However, such is the demand for the Norfolk product, that a number of other sources are being exploited and Mr Barrett now gets as much Hampshire reed (*spear*) as he can from various inlets along the coast.

Reed is supplied to the thatcher in bundles from 3-9 ft long and measuring about 27 in round at a foot above the butt. Before use, any remaining flag is cleaned out (another bad weather job) and the bundles are *knocked up* on a board or smooth surface to bring the butts level. It is also graded so that the longest reed can be used on the large main areas of the roof and the shortest at the ridge. Norfolk reed is hung butt downwards after the ties of the bundles have been cut.

The bundles of reed are held down by $\frac{1}{4}$ in steel reinforcing rods tied to the rafters with polypropylene twine, and the reed's natural taper allows it to be driven tight under. (An older method was to use hazel rods pinned to the rafters by long pointed iron *crooks*.) A *bittle* (called in many areas a *leggett*) is used for this job, which is a square elm bat with a short handle, its beating surface set with projecting horseshoe nails in diagonal

*The finished capping, held securely and decoratively in place with 'diamond work'. Bent, twisted spars are used like clothes' pegs to hold the ledgers.*

rows. It is constantly in the thatcher's hand for dressing the reed up the roof slope and along eaves and round dormers; to leave ridges or joins showing anywhere is regarded as a sign of poor work, only worthy of some incompetent *straw hanger*. A horizontal lining of loose reed is packed under the bundles, in order to present a tidy appearance when the roof is seen from the inside. Reed thatching goes on the roof in horizontal *sets*, which means that it is often necessary to have rather large sections exposed in the course of work.

As previously mentioned, reed cannot be used for the ridge, and sedge, cut in the summer before it has ripened and become unpleasantly sharp to handle, is normally used. In maturing, it changes colour to a pleasant brown which blends well with the reed. If very dry it may have to be dampened and made up into yealms like long straw.

When the reed nears the ridge of the roof, a dolly of about 6 in diameter is tied along the ridge board so that the reed lies against it on either side. The ends of the reed are trimmed off and the sedge laid over. Depending on how sharp a ridge the thatcher wants to make, further dollies and layers of sedge may be required, each being well sparred in. A cresting is often

*Norfolk reed is delivered to the thatcher in bundles which must be knocked up to level the butts before being hung. Reed may be even taller than this – up to 9 ft. Notice the knee pads, a necessary protection when so much time is spent leaning from ladders.*

worked above gables and here some thatchers add a 'trade mark' or device by way of decoration: crowns, cockerels, pheasants and pinnacles are sometimes seen, but their life is rather short. Sedge is generally used to complete any junction with a chimney, after which the lead flashing is laid. Norfolk reed is held with decorative sparring only along the ridge, which is usually trimmed with scallops or tongues like long-straw work.

Combed wheat reed has much in common with Norfolk reed as far as application and appearance are concerned but a lot depends on the preparation of the straw if its reed-like quality is to be kept. The old varieties, with stalks as much as 3 ft tall, produced something very much like a miniature reed and it is still necessary to have tall varieties to put through the comber. This is an attachment fitted to a threshing machine which strips the flag and most of the ears off the straw and ejects it as reed, the butts all one way, when it is passed to a tier to be bundled. The straw must be carefully fed by hand into the comber.

*An ovis knife being used to trim the eaves of a cottage thatched with long-straw; a pair of sheep shears are to hand just above for any tidying-up. On a summer's day the thatcher's life seems an enviable one, but it is less so in the winter months.*

When he receives the bundles, the thatcher first butts them to bring the ends level, trimming them if necessary, and then up-ends them to be watered and lays them down to soak. Thereafter, work proceeds much as for Norfolk reed. A slightly different kind of bittle is used for dressing, faced with parallel grooves instead of nails. In addition, the finished surface may be trimmed down with a sickle-like *shearing hook*. An *ovis knife* with a short handle and slightly curved blade about 34 in long, is used to trim off eaves and gables.

When the top of the roof is reached, it is usual to build up a pattern course with a roll to which the reed is sparred in on either side. A narrow ridge may be built up as with Norfolk reed, with the difference that wheat reed, being more flexible, can be used throughout. Long bunches, packed tight, are laid over for the final course, the ridge is secured with spars and the pattern cut.

The thatcher's final task on any roof is to cover it with fine-mesh wire netting, paying attention to neat joins – not to hold the thatch on but to keep out the birds and mice that can do so much damage. It is no deterrent to the bees and wasps who sometimes penetrate old thatch and build inside.

To see a thatcher pulling off old thatch, with a great crackling bonfire blazing nearby, does not necessarily mean that the roof is being stripped down to the bare bones. Often, thatch that is rotting on the surface is sound enough below and with long-straw and combed wheat reed the undercoat can be retained and a new top coat sparred into it. A roof that has been re-coated several times may have acquired a great thickness of thatch and it is not uncommon for as much as five or six feet to be removed. With Norfolk reed, it is the ridge which is most likely to decay and re-placement frequently gives the whole thing a new lease of life.

The cost of a thatching job is based on the *square* of 100 square feet. Norfolk reed and combed wheat reed cost more than twice as much a square as long-straw, but this must be looked at in the light of their relative durability: long-straw 12-20 years, combed wheat reed 25-40 years, Norfolk reed 50-60 years. About half of Mr Barrett's work is in long-straw. He reckons that on average he can manage about a square a day.

When Mr Barrett left school his first job was on a farm, but he only stuck it for a short time before being given what he now sees as a providential stroke of good fortune, a trial as a thatcher's assistant. He discovered an aptitude for the job and found, almost without realising it, that work had been transformed from being just a means of earning money into a way of life. Now, years later, everything about reed and straw continues to fascinate him; among his hobbies is making corn dollies of meticulous finish; he even sports a beard that looks like nothing so much as a piece of well-laid long-straw. He takes a lively interest in the life of the countryside, claiming that his own contribution lies in having 'the most photographed backside in Hampshire'. To Mr Barrett and men of his calling, lovers of the countryside owe much, for his craft is one of the remaining few that directly influence the quality of the rural environment.

# The wood turner

Some of the craftsmen whose work is described in other chapters are well known locally, one or two even nationally, and most of them have many years' experience behind them; so it seems only right that by way of contrast we should include an account of a newcomer to the scene. Brian Healey is a wood turner: a somewhat unusual occupation, for although plenty of people enjoy turning as a hobby there are very few earning a living from it. That is not to say that there is no longer a call for turnery; but automatic turning machines do most of the repetition work for industry, such as making tool handles and furniture parts, and plastics provide a cheap and convenient alternative to wood for a host of small things. No doubt domestic fashions, too, have been partly accountable for a decline in the craft over the past fifty years – the average house once contained far more turnery than it does today.

Mr Healey grew up with a liking for woodwork and handicrafts and took up turning as a hobby, years before ever thinking about it as a livelihood. He was born in Leeds between the wars, trained as a mechanical engineer and went into the quarrying industry. At the age of 25 he became a quarry manager and in due course was managing a group of nine quarries in the northeast. Apparently set for a career in management, he found himself beset by a growing unease about his way of life: the separateness of his position seemed unreal, and likewise the attitude of deference shown by men who worked with their hands but whose years of practical experience made them every bit his equals. Perhaps time would eventually have blunted the edge of Mr Healey's disquiet, but then a personal crisis precipitated a desire for change and led him to throw up his job, move south and see if he could earn a living with his hands. So it happened that early in 1973 he found himself at North Baddesley, facing a new and uncertain future, and the challenge of making a name for himself as a professional wood turner.

Challenge is perhaps the key word in turning, since the craftsman, un-

*Turning lends itself to the production of a wide variety of useful and attractive goods, which are frequently enhanced by the revelation of the grain.*

like other woodworkers, is restricted by the limited way his work can be manipulated and a rather small range of tool types. What makes turning different, is that the workpiece moves in relation to the tool rather than the tool being brought to act upon the workpiece. Because the workpiece is rotating it follows that all shaping creates circular profiles, though cuts made at right-angles to the axis will produce flat surfaces.

Basically, there are two kinds of turning: *between-centres work* and *faceplate work*. In the former, the workpiece is held between the *headstock* and *tailstock* centres of the lathe while revolving; long shapes such as legs, lampstands and handles are made in this way, their maximum length depending on the adjustment of the tailstock along the *bed* of the lathe. Several small items such as drawer pulls or bobbins can be turned together on the same length of wood and then parted.

In faceplate work, the workpiece is screwed to a metal disc or faceplate on the headstock spindle. On many lathes the spindle projects outwards beyond the lathe bed and a large workpiece can be turned without obstruction from the bed; Mr Healey's lathe has a headstock that turns through 90° to achieve the same result. Items requiring hollowing, or

66

having flat circular surfaces, such as bowls, platters and mirror frames are made on the faceplate.

The characteristic production shapes of the two methods have given rise to the names by which they are most easily remembered: *spindle turning* and *bowl turning*.

The turner employs three main groups of tools. Those most frequently in his hands are the gouges, often known by reason of their length and stoutness as *long and strong gouges;* their blades may be 12 in long and handles another 14 in. The blade is of very thick section, deep or shallow fluted according to function: the U-shaped kind is used for bowl turning, the half-round kind for spindle turning. A gouge is sharpened with a steep bevel which acts as a resting angle against the workpiece, the blade being held on the tool rest by one hand, the long handle against the thigh by the other. It is controlled by gently levering up or down. Gouges are always used with the bevel rubbing a little above the centre of the work in order to avoid the possibility of digging in – the most frequent cause of disaster and injury to the careless. The value of the fluted section lies in allowing the tool to be used with a rolling action, so facilitating work within hollows and presenting plenty of edge to the wood (tools blunt quickly and the turner is continually re-sharpening them). Gouges used in small hollows have the business end of the blade curved like a finger nail, so the corners are less likely to dig in.

The second group of tools consists of the *long and strong chisels*, whose main use is in finishing straight turning. There are two kinds, *straight-across chisels* and *long-eared chisels* with oblique blades. Turning chisels are readily distinguished from carpentry chisels by having generally wider blades with hollow-ground bevels on both faces; as with gouges, the bevels act as rubbing or resting edges. Chisels are used angled towards the upper part of the workpiece, taking care that the trailing corners do not dig in. Related to the chisels is the *parting tool*, used for cutting beadings and details and for separating finished work from waste ends. It resembles a narrow chisel, with long bevels on each face and waisted sides which remain clear of the wood when making deep cuts.

Then there are *scrapers*, long-handled and rather like chisels, with straight, oblique or curved edges ground to a steep bevel. They are used for obtaining a fine finish on bowl turning, and are angled below the centre line of the work so that the burr of the bevel has a scraping effect. Most turners make a few non-standard scrapers to their own liking out of old files or planing machine blades.

A characteristic piece of spindle turning for Mr Healey is a table lamp – 12 in × 4 in is a useful size. Selecting a seasoned piece of square timber just over the required size, he first finds the centres by drawing diagonal

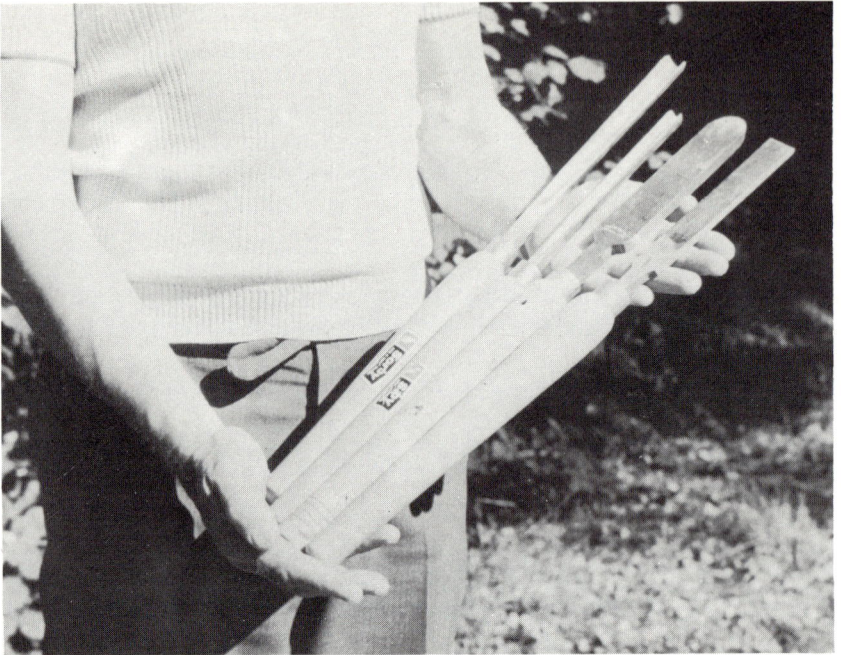

*The remarkable length of the wood turner's tools allows a delicate and precise leverage against the rotating workpiece. Seen here, from the left, are two deep-fluted gouges, a scraper and a chisel.*

lines across each end, and where they intersect he makes a hole with a square-sectioned *birdcage awl*. These are the positions for the lathe centres. The wood is gently tapped onto the driving centre to locate it, then the tailstock centre, lightly greased, is screwed up tight to the other end and eased off slightly so that the work will rotate smoothly.

Amateurs like to plane off the corners of the wood before starting to turn, but the maker who handles his tools with confidence can eliminate this step. He sets the tool rest so that it clears the wood when turned over by hand (a preliminary safety precaution) and starts work with a series of short cuts at one end, and then works along the length of the wood to round it. An inch-wide *roughing-out gouge* is used at this stage. With the body of the lamp roughed out, salient details of the design are marked off with a pencil. If several are being made to the same design, a marked length of wood is used as a guide and callipers are used to check their diameters. Deep parts of the design are cut with the parting tool or a chisel on edge and are rounded off with a smaller gouge; a $\frac{3}{8}$ in gouge is Mr Healey's favourite. The very fine ribbing left by the gouge is removed with a chisel, then the piece is given a fine finish with sandpaper before oiling or waxing. The flex hole is drilled by passing a long auger through a special hollow tail centre, stopping just short of the end. A second hole is then bored from the side of the base to meet it. It takes about half an hour to make such a lamp.

Bowl turning is considered to be the real test of a turner's skill. The bottom is done first, while the means of attachment to the faceplate – the waste interior – is still available. Then the work is turned over and the finished base screwed to the faceplate. Now the turner has to begin hollowing out, and here a steady hand is necessary to ensure that the gouge enters without wavering or jumping and rolls smoothly from side to side on the bevel. The gouge sings quietly to the accompaniment of the lathe motor as it edges into the wood and a shower of shavings settles on the turner's hands and in his hair. As the gouge goes gradually deeper, the value of the deep, fluted U section is seen in allowing it to work in a confined space without corners to dig in. After the main work has been done, scrapers are called into play for smoothing off, and for any shaping where it might not be possible to handle a gouge. When Mr Healey has several smallish repetition pieces to make on the faceplate it is sometimes worth his while to make a special wooden chuck to hold the bases. This is just a shallow flanged disc, whose internal diameter tightly fits the foot of the article being made; it goes on the faceplate and eliminates the need for screws and screw holes in the workpiece.

Several finishes can be applied to turnery. The simplest is burnishing the revolving work with a handful of shavings; the most attractive is beeswax and turpentine; but the quickest and most effective for a great many jobs is a quick-drying friction polish which melts into the wood. Teak is usually oiled, and salad bowls are finished with olive oil. Most turners abhor the use of stains, rightly claiming that nothing should be allowed to obscure the natural beauty of the grain.

Getting the timber he needs is a problem Mr Healey experiences like other woodworkers. While almost any wood can be turned (though softwoods can be tricky), the native English hardwoods are especially desirable. Beech, walnut, sycamore and elm are all good for use with food, having a neutral taste, but are in short supply. He has to rely heavily on imported teak, afrormosia, iroko, utile and sapele. But the problem may not be just one of getting the right timber, but of getting it in small quantities, and Mr Healey is always looking out for usable offcuts. The small sawmills that once abounded are now few, and today's big firms are readier to supply a lorry-load of hardwood than the odd plank. Seasoning is important, too: green timber turns easily but soon warps. However, the old rule of thumb about allowing timber to season one year for every inch of thickness can be helped along by rough-turning the work down to about an inch and thus saving two years on a dish three inches deep.

A much bigger problem is that of becoming established as a craftsman: attracting customers, finding sales outlets, learning what people will buy and what are the right prices to ask. Shops tend to demand too large a profit margin and Mr Healey feels that it is not worth trying to compete with the low-priced (and often poor quality) machine turnery which appears in the big stores. A more helpful attitude and more discriminating customers are found in the craft galleries. For a time, he set up shop in his small caravan in Lymington market each Saturday, working away at his wood carving – animals, abstracts, name plates – while waiting for customers looking for unusual handmade gifts. Listening to the remarks of people who thought hand work ought to cost no more than moulded plastic was a traumatic experience at times, but a sense of humour enabled him to see that it may have been a salutary one as well. After that, he found a more congenial atmosphere working in a nearby craft centre.

Determination is slowly bringing results. As his work has become known, Mr Healey has received commissions to undertake restoration work, has been asked to make fittings and carvings for a luxury boat, and has taken part in various craft shows and commercial exhibitions. He is always on the lookout for new things to make and new ideas about turnery design. His work covers a wide range: bowls, platters, goblets, lamps, teapot stands, reel holders, barometers, canisters, butter dishes, wine tables and stools. Even the humble toilet roll holder achieves a new quality at his hands.

It is not really appropriate to ask if Mr Healey, having ventured all on a new way of life, is making a success of it. Success is a relative thing, and at this stage it means being able to keep body and soul together through the work of his own hands; at some future time it could well mean the setting up of a combined shop and workshop somewhere in the New Forest. One thing is certain – he is finding fulfilment, and that is something every craftsman needs.

# SPORTING CRAFTS

# The bowyer

It is one of the ironies of history that archery, once encouraged and even enjoined by statute as vital for the defence of the realm, has declined to the position of one of the less common sports, and a rather expensive one at that. The bow, among the most ancient of weapons, has played a crucial part in many decisive battles: we hardly need reminding of the Norman archers at Hastings, or the English ones at Crécy and Agincourt. It could truthfully be asserted that the long bow has had a hand in shaping the course of English history.

Coming across a bowyer at work in these modern times may therefore induce a mild pleasurable thrill in anyone with a sense of historical continuity, for here is a living link with the ancient, legendary past. But Lew Smith, at work in his quiet corner of the village of Sopley, has both feet firmly planted in the present, maintaining his reputation as one of a small number of professional bow makers. It is a reputation won the hard way, beginning in the days when he first attempted to make his own bows because he could not afford to buy them. The craft demands a high degree of accuracy and it is quite likely that his engineering background helped him to make a precise and methodical approach to it. What started as a hobby eventually became too compelling to resist and Mr Smith got a job with a firm of bow makers. After that it was only a step to branching out on his own, and for over eighteen years now he has been one of that band of craftsmen who cater for the rapidly expanding sport and leisure market. His workshop was once the village wheelwright's shop and still keeps its long side windows with their overlapping panes which let the sunlight stream in.

No bow that is worth having is quickly made. Mr Smith turns out three in a week but emphasises that he could easily spend a fortnight on a single one if he was aiming for a high degree of perfection; perhaps it is that kind of striving after really high quality that accounts in part for his difficulty in getting apprentice help of the right sort. But that is a problem he shares

*Two or more woods of contrasting colour may be used to build up the riser of a composite bow. The basic assembly is seen on top, and below is a similar bow after shaping and attachment of the glass-fibre limbs.*

with many of today's craftsmen. Bows needing to be tailor-made for champions allow him the luxury of a little more time.

The kind of long bow which the English yeoman took to France is not much used by serious archers today, since changing technology has allowed considerable improvements to be made. The old type of bow was basically a long stave of skilfully split and shaved yew wood with a hand-grip a little below the centre point, the whole thing forming a huge spring. Today's *composite bow* is markedly different in appearance, consisting of an elaborately-shaped centre section or *riser*, often laminated in two or more woods, to which are attached re-curved *limbs* of laminated glass fibre. The theory of this type of bow is that the substantial riser will help absorb the torque created in the limbs when they are flexed and so make for steadier and more accurate release of arrows. Stabilising rods can be screwed into many bows with a view to correcting lateral torque. (They project from the *back*, the side opposite the *belly* which is towards the user.) An archer from the time of Agincourt would probably think the whole thing quite extraordinary, but then it has been developed by an application of scientific principles and techniques which were quite unknown in his day.

Several timbers are popular for bow making. Mr Smith's likings are all for imported ones, such as American walnut, padouk, bubinga and rose-wood – the last is especially sought after. In cheaper bows the riser may be made from one piece of wood only, whereas in most better ones it is built up, often using two woods separated by thin laminations of another with contrasting colour, such as Canadian rock maple. A combination of rose wood and walnut makes for a particularly rich effect. But fine timbers are not always easy to get hold of and there have been times when Mr Smith has been reduced to buying up old furniture for the sake of the wood!

Making a bow begins with gluing up the accurately-machined pieces of wood which have been selected for the riser. This produces a somewhat irregular, oversize block that can be cut to shape after the profiles have been marked out with the aid of templates. Cutting is done with a bandsaw and a spindle moulder.

To this riser section must be attached the limbs of glass fibre, each consisting of two strap-like pieces with a thin core of wood. Upon the construction of the limbs the *draw weight* of the bow largely depends; that, in simple terms, is the number of pounds which, attached to the centre of the string, would equal the owner's full draw. It ranges from about 32 lb - 42 lb for men's bows and about 26 lb - 34 lb for women's bows. *Male* and *female* formers, cut to a predetermined curve, are held together by metal U-clamps with the glued limb laminations between; at the same time, the parted inner ends of the limbs are glued to the tapering ends of the riser so that the whole thing becomes one structure. Gluing is speeded by placing the whole bow in a *warm box*. As Mr Smith makes a range of bows, he needs to have pairs of formers and sets of templates for each model, and they hang on one wall of the workshop, marked with their various names: 'Otter', 'Heron', 'Flamingo' and so on.

Thus far Mr Smith would probably regard the job as straightforward enough, but he knows that the real skill lies in finishing a bow, and that is the finicky and time-consuming part. He has to work a handle with pistol grip, and above that a cutaway *sight window* which gives arrow clearance and allows the archer to take clear aim. Upon the carefully-thought-out design of the grip depends the bow's balance and comfort in the user's hand, and consequently much of its performance. *Nocks* for the string are worked at the tip of each limb and so angled that they will cause the minimum amount of chafing. Nothing elaborate in the way of tools is called for at this stage – chiefly Surform tools, files and sandpaper, wrapped round various blocks or rods to get into awkward places. More important are an experienced eye and plenty of patience.

With polishing, the bow takes on its finished appearance. Mr Smith may put on and rub down as many as a dozen coats of polyurethane

*A bow is wedged against its maker's instep while he slips the string over the nock. When correctly tensioned, the string should be the space of a fist with outstretched thumb away from the handle (the fistmele).*

varnish before he is satisfied that the look of the thing, as well as its construction, will do him credit. And after that kind of care and attention, is it any wonder that he feels he has put something of himself into each of his bows? He reflects about his work: 'You've got to have a little poetry in your soul . . . You just can't make it and say "That's it – I've finished it".' Naturally, he takes a keen interest in the subsequent performance of his bows and gets great satisfaction from learning when they have done well.

There is one last thing that has to be done before a bow goes into service, and that is to make and fit the string. Traditional linen thread has given way to Dacron, *served* (bound) at the loops and *nocking point* (where the arrow nock engages) with nylon. The correct length of the string when the bow is braced is that which achieves *fistmele:* an old term meaning the width of a clenched fist placed on the handle with thumb outstretched. The tip should just touch the string. The bowyer's craft today may seem a far cry from what it was when the bow was a national weapon, until

76

some such word crops up; then for a moment an ancient echo sounds and links our modern enthusiast with his forebears of 1388, when Richard II enacted that, 'Servants and Labourers shall have bows and arrows, and use the same the Sundays and holydays, and leave all playing at tennis or football . . . and other such importune games.'

# The farrier

Everyone knows when Rodney Downer is in because his presence is advertised by the insistent ringing of his hammer, coming from a corner of the stable yard. It is the anvil music of an ancient skill, a purposeful yet melodious sound which progress has inevitably denied to most modern ears, though it was once commonplace. Those living before the Second World War, however, will recall the forges to be found in most villages and many back streets, where horses stood patiently, lifting a ponderous hoof on demand for the shoe to be seated amid a cloud of acrid smoke. They will remember the begrimed smith in his leather apron, the glowing hearth and the dancing hammer working iron into shape; and perhaps they will sigh for his passing. Now the horse has gone from our fields and streets and the farrier, or shoeing-smith, survives on the business created by training stables, riding schools and pony lovers.

As a consequence of changed times, farriers are today somewhat thinly scattered, and where it is not practical to bring horses to the forge, the farrier must be prepared to travel to his customers. Some have ingeniously organised travelling forges in vans and run a kind of 'flying farrier' service; others, like Mr Downer, work for a group of stables – four in his case. His forge is at a racehorse training stable at Littleton, but, even here, no horse actually comes to him to be shod since he keeps patterns from which to make new shoes for cold fitting with on-the-spot adjustments. Thus he has a ready reference for every horse on his books and can work uninterruptedly on shoe production.

Some farriers buy in ready-made shoes to adjust as required, but not so Mr Downer, who makes his entirely, working with easy skill born of more than forty years' practice (he was apprenticed at Fordingbridge at the age of fourteen, serving four years with a further two as an improver). He begins a shoe by selecting and cutting off a length of mild steel bar, supplied ready *fullered* with the groove which will later accommodate the nail heads. The metal comes in various sizes, ranging from $\frac{5}{8} \times \frac{3}{8}$ in for ponies to $\frac{3}{4} \times \frac{1}{2}$ in for hunters and $\frac{7}{8} \times \frac{1}{2}$ in for heavy cobs, with a few other sizes in between. Racehorses mostly have light $\frac{5}{8} \times \frac{5}{16}$ in shoes for exercising and very light steel or aluminium *plates* for the course. The rule of thumb for length of bar is 'twice the width of the foot plus an inch', though like all such rules it must be applied intelligently. After marking the length, the bar is cut by placing it groove down over an old triangular file on the anvil and giving it a few smart blows. Then the piece is centred by balancing on the file and is given a tap to mark it.

When he has cut two bars – because he likes to make shoes in pairs, front first – Mr Downer turns to his hearth, switches on the electric blower and pushes the two lengths into the fire, heaping up the fine coal with his *slice*. In a few moments they are glowing orange-red and he can switch off the blower and pick out one piece with the tongs. He starts the shaping with two or three taps to bend the bar at a right angle, *knocks off* the roughness of the heel at one end and shapes that half into a curve over the *beak* of the anvil. Working rapidly before the heat goes, he uses a square-section punch to make the first group of holes, measuring off by eye about an inch from the centre mark and an inch between holes. Punching is done from the grooved side, over the *punch hole* on the anvil, and the tapered holes so made are deepened with a long, spike-like *pritchel*. The shoe is now cooling, so it is *levelled off* by hammering against the anvil top to put right any swelling caused by the curving operation and the holes are cleaned out with the pritchel from the underside. Then it goes back into the fire while the first half of the other shoe is made. That done, the sequence of heating, shaping, punching and levelling is repeated to complete the second half of both shoes, with the punch being dipped in water from time to time to preserve its temper. There is, of course, a difference in the two sides of a horseshoe: there are four holes on the outside, three holes on the inside. That is the usual practice, but Mr Downer makes five and four respectively, because many of his horses are reshod at short intervals for racing work and strain on their hooves can be lessened by varying the holes in use.

Although the shoes so far made could be worn, and worn quite usefully, two details have yet to be completed for them to be most effective: bevelling the heels and making the clips which project from the top surface. The heel ends of the shoes have a square-edged profile that could cause cuts on the hind legs in a gallop, so Mr Downer reduces them by hammering into a home-made bevelling tool fitted into the square *hardie hole* in the tail of the anvil.

Clips do not appear to have been made before the nineteenth century, although they seem an obvious way of lessening the risk of shoes working back along the foot. The usual practice is to make one clip in the centre

*The farrier uses two tools to make the nail holes in a horseshoe, a short punch and a tapering pritchel (on right of anvil). Here the holes are receiving a final clean-up. Notice the deep fullering in which the nail heads will seat and the carefully-trimmed heel ends of the shoes.*

of fore-shoes and two rather to the sides of hind-shoes, remembering again the risk of cuts. When the centre of the shoe is re-heated for knocking out the clip, the full use of the farrier's *catshead* hammer is seen. So far, the two end faces, flat or convex, have been used; now the webs on the sides come into play. The shoe is held against the side of the anvil away from the maker and the pointed web is used to knock the clip out roughly; then the hammer is turned over and the ridged web used to finish the job.

Mr Downer works with an amazing deftness which would delight a time-and-motion researcher, and in a gloomy light most people would find intolerable. But the poor light is curiously useful, as it enables him to see the colour of his hot metal and judge its state for working. The same holds good in any blacksmith's shop.

And here the difference between 'blacksmith' and 'farrier' ought to be explained since the names are often used indiscriminately. A farrier may reasonably be referred to as 'the blacksmith' since a good grounding in smithing techniques is essential to him, but a blacksmith may not neces-

*Knocking out a clip over the edge of the anvil; this is the function of the two webs on the sides of the catshead hammer. Front shoes have one clip, rear shoes two, and they prevent sliding back along the foot.*

sarily have the training needed for shoeing horses. Years ago, the terms were synonymous but today, with the specialised training courses and qualifications open to aspiring farriers the distinction has become clearer. Farriers are justifiably proud of their calling, for what other craftsman practises on living creatures and combines the skills of a metalworker and a vet? He must know a great deal about the anatomy and diseases of the horse's leg and how good shoeing can prevent or cure faults of *action*. Older farriers have been known to speak of vets in unguarded moments with something approaching scorn, such is their jealous regard for inherited wisdom.

It goes without saying that a farrier needs a real love of horses to be successful, and Mr Downer soon comes to an understanding of those he deals with. He knows, for example, that racehorses can be highly strung and need careful handling, and that no horse should be approached without warning. 'If I get one that's very nervous, I always go in and talk to it before I do anything to it . . . I let it get to know me.' So confidence is built up.

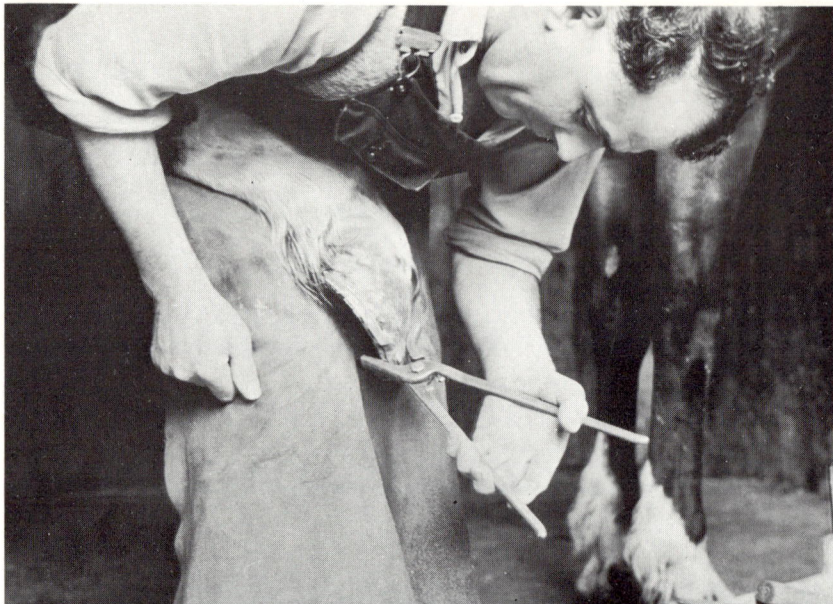

*A relaxed but confident approach by the farrier helps the horse to respond calmly when being shod. The job is almost finished as the projecting clinches are turned over with special tongs.*

Nor must the farrier be nervous. A few soothing words, a hand run firmly down the appropriate leg, and the foot is lifted to be held steady on Mr Downer's leather apron. With his *buffer* he knocks off the turned-over *clinches* of the old nails so that the shoe can be lifted with the pincers, nails and all, starting at the heel and gradually lifting up all round. Then, reversing his position so the underside of the foot can be raised, he uses a *hoof knife* or pincer-like *hoof cutters* to trim the hoof, taking care not to remove any of the central *frog* which presses against the ground and creates proper muscular action. A nick is taken out at the front for the clip to fit into and the hoof smoothed off with a rasp.

All necessary tools are kept handy in a small raised box with a tray at one end for nails. Some kind of portable anvil is desirable for cold shoeing, which relies on careful levelling of shoe and foot, so Mr Downer takes round with him part of an old wagon axle on which to do any hammering (hot shoeing can only be done at a forge where the shoe can be heated for seating). It is important for the shoe to bear evenly on the wall of the foot all round.

Nails, used in varying sizes according to the shoe dimensions, are driven outwards through the wall of the hoof and then pulled downwards and

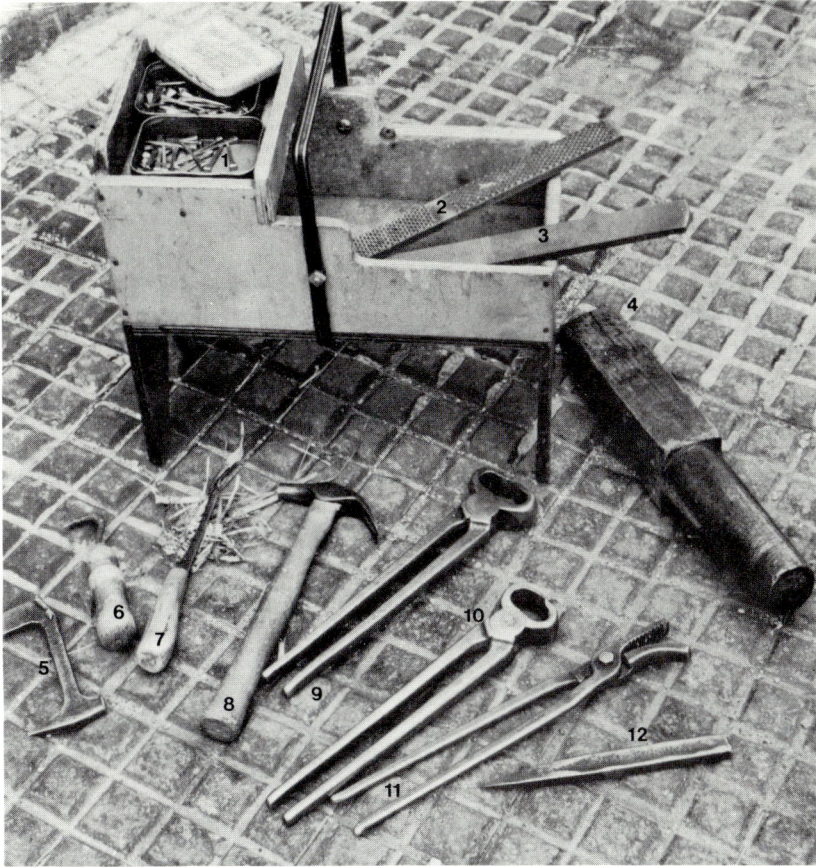

*In his box the farrier keeps everything needed for the actual work of shoeing. Although recently made, it follows the time-honoured pattern.*

*(1) Nails (2) Rasp (3) File (4) Old axle stub: serves as portable anvil (5) Buffer: removes old clinches (6) Hoof pick (7) Hoof knife (8) Shoeing hammer (9) Pincers (10) Hoof cutter (11) Clinching tongs (12) Pritchel: for enlarging nail holes.*

twisted off with the pincers to leave a short stub; the pincers' jaws are held against this and the nail driven up tight. After filing off any rough ends, the clinches are turned down into the hoof using American *clinching tongs*. Mr Downer likes this better than the old method of hammering onto the hoof wall.

Examination of a shoeing nail, square-sectioned with long point and tapering head, shows why the holes were so carefully countersunk into the shoe: use only presses the nails in more securely and cannot remove their heads, so the shoe is firmly held for its life. The fullered groove helps to protect the heads and also reduces slipping. It was not considered necessary for heavy agricultural shoes.

As late as the 1950s, Mr Downer's concern was chiefly with working horses and sadly it is a rarity now to come across a farmer who still uses them. But he has vivid memories of the old days in the countryside when the horse and its well-being were still vital to a great deal of activity and there might be as many as eight horses at a time in the forge:

> 'When I started there was, well, the butcher, the baker, the grocer, they all had horses and used to drive round. And I used to get up at six o'clock in the morning, and go down to the butcher's stable or the baker's stable and collect the horse, and bring it back to the forge and get it shod, and take it back again before they were ready to go out on their rounds. And then we used to go to the farms in the mornings at about half past six and shoe the horses before they went out to plough in the mornings. We used to make the shoes back at the forge and take them with us. You always kept a pattern. The only days that you got the horses in the forge would be a wet day, when they couldn't go to work on the land. If you had to alter a carthorse shoe you had quite a job on when it was $1\frac{1}{4}$ in-wide metal and about $\frac{1}{2}$ in thick. One horse that we used to shoe, it used to take 6 ft 4 in of $1\frac{1}{4} \times \frac{5}{8}$ in to make him a set of shoes!'

Today, although things are so different, Rodney Downer continues to be busy because he has been able to transfer his skill without difficulty to a fresh scene, the booming leisure business. Indeed, with racehorses needing to be shod at least three times a month and before every race, the demands on his services are considerable. So his future seems assured and the craft will surely flourish. But his calling is one which deserves our interest for another reason, since it is among the last surviving links with that im-memorial era which ended not so long ago, when man depended on the horse as one of his chief sources of motive power, and man and horse worked the land in partnership.

# The fly dresser

One of the smallest craft products made anywhere is undoubtedly that created by the hands of Jackie Wakeford of Romsey, who is one of the country's few full-time professional fly dressers: that is, she makes the artificial insects used as a means of enticement by fly fishermen. It is delicate work, calling for deftness and patience and for no little understanding of the angler's problems. But before looking at the ways in which flies are used and their materials of manufacture, a word of history may be found interesting, as the technique of catching fish with an artificial insect is older than many fishermen perhaps realise.

The earliest-known description of a fishing fly occurs in the works of the Greek, Claudius Aelian, dating from about AD 200, so it can be assumed that the practice is considerably older. The first English description of a group of flies is found in the quaintly-titled 'Treatyse of Fysshynge with an Angle' written early in the fifteenth century and printed by Wynkyn de Worde in the *Boke of St Albans*, 1496. Nothing further on the subject appeared until a handful of works was published in the second half of the seventeenth century, the most celebrated being Izaak Walton's *Compleat Angler* (1653) which has become both a fishing and a literary classic. But the sport of fly fishing continued to gain popularity, and by the end of the nineteenth century many books, some beautifully illustrated, had been written to show how the making and use of flies derived from careful observation of real insects.

Thus, the fisherman found that he needed to be something of an entomologist, with a sport calling for the exercise of finesse, and leisure in which to acquire it. An important part of that finesse was ability in making flies and it came to be recognised as one of the skills proper to the complete country gentleman. A great body of lore grew up round the tying and casting of flies and the mystique continues to this day to the delight of devotees and the confusion of the uninitiated. There are now many thousands of patterns for flies, derived from the different stages of insect life, the supposed appeal to the fish of various insect features, and, by no means least important, their appeal to the fisherman's fancy. However, it is enough to point out here that the great majority are used in catching trout or salmon and can be classed in four groups.

*Dry flies* represent floating insects such as mayflies or gnats and great attention is paid to producing a lifelike imitation. Good balance and buoyancy are essential as they are fished on the surface. In some patterns the treatment of the wings is paramount, in others the *hackle* (feather fibres) which supports the fly on the water surface.

*Wet flies* represent emerging pupae and drowned flies. They are fished underwater and must be dressed on a sufficiently heavy hook to submerge. Considerable reality is aimed at but colours are rather bright so they can be seen in the water.

*Nymphs* represent various kinds of larvae and small water creatures. Again, desirable qualities are to sink quickly and to bear a good likeness to the profile of the original.

*Salmon flies* are really lures and do not represent actual creatures. They are fished underwater, and in some cases their structure streams out to look rather like a small fish, but for the most part they are simply bright attractors designed to tempt the fish in water that is often clouded. They adhere strictly to classic patterns but may be dressed in various sizes.

The chief material of the fly dresser's stock-in-trade is feathers, and Miss Wakeford's diminutive workshop contains a large assortment, displayed on shelves in glass jars and filed in envelopes in drawers. With their subtle markings and varied colours – some bright, others muted – they are a delight to the eye, and their names read like an aviary catalogue. A large proportion come from the many species of poultry, pheasant and duck. Tail, wing, breast and neck or hackle feathers are most commonly used, the latter often obtained still attached to the skin in *capes*. Miss Wakeford gets her feathers from specialist suppliers, so it is not surprising that the amateur fly tyer sometimes finds it difficult to manage if he is restricted to the feathers he can find. One book on fly dressing lists forty-five birds whose various feathers are used in trout flies and thirty-one others in salmon flies; among them are such exotics as ibis, macaw and condor. Many of the specified feathers are hard to get and substitutes have to be used; even suitable poultry feathers can be hard to come by these days as cockerels are killed off before their plumage matures at about two years old. Some of the brightest feathers on Miss Wakeford's shelves are in fact dyed to meet the particular requirements of salmon flies.

Other materials used include certain furs (seal, mole, and hare, for example) for making bodies, tying silk of various colours, beeswax, gilt and silver tinsel of different widths, and varnish for sealing the tying silk

*Fly dressing takes up less room than any other craft, but the professional has to be well organised. Good eyesight, deftness and infinite patience are the chief qualifications for practitioners of this delicate work.*

to prevent it unwinding. The fly dresser's tools are few, the most necessary being a light vice to hold the hook while the fly is being made; a lever-operated one with a pointed collet nose can be used for both small and large hooks. Next, there are fine scissors, straight and curved, a *dubbing needle* which may be just a domestic one set in a piece of dowel, and *hackle pliers* of small and medium size. These are light spring clamps with a neatly closing jaw used to hold hackle feathers when winding them round fly bodies. A pair of tweezers and a penknife complete Miss Wakeford's equipment, though further accessories can be employed.

A description of the tying of two well-known flies, one simple, the other complicated, will serve to illustrate some of the fly dresser's terms and techniques. The first is a trout dry fly, the Black Gnat. It is made on a size 14, standard pattern, wide-gape, up-eyed trout hook, i.e., it is $\frac{11}{32}$ in long, excluding the eye which is turned away from the barb, and the latter is well apart from the shank. The hook is placed in the tip of the vice so that the point does not project. Black tying silk is used and a length from the bobbin is run across the beeswax to improve its adhesion. Starting

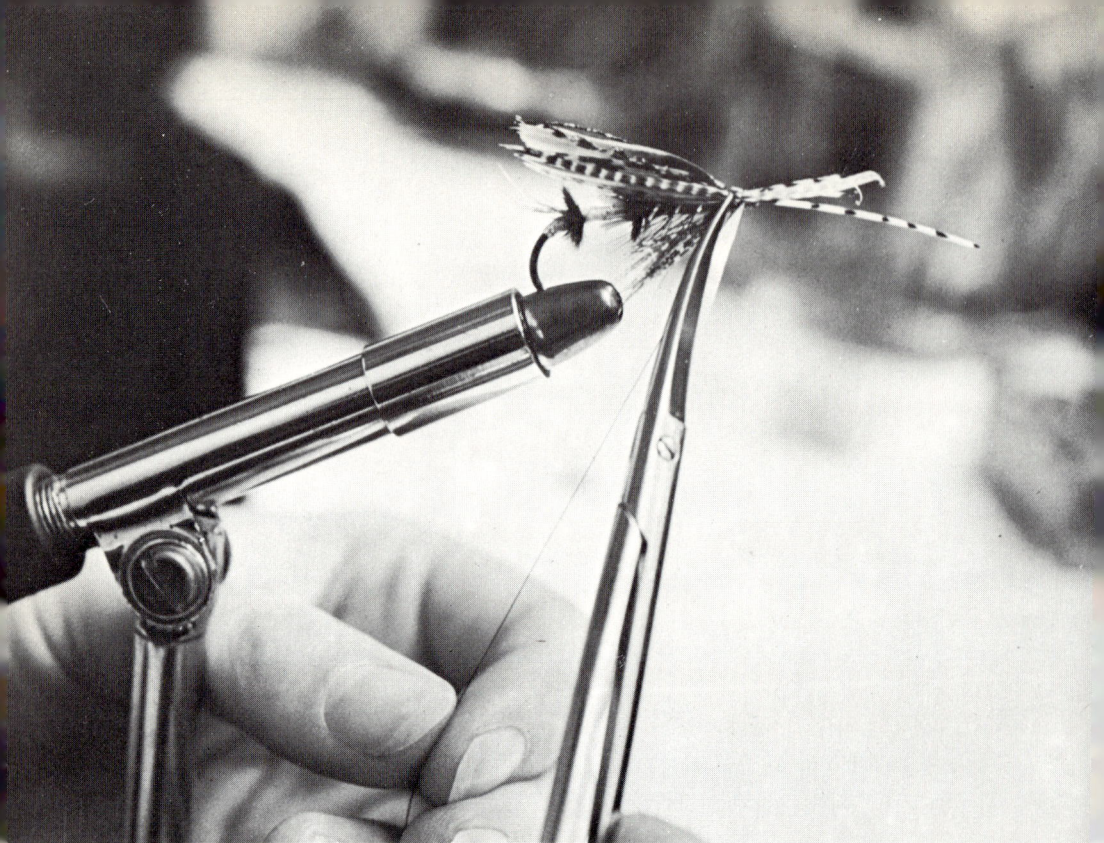

*A Jock Scott salmon fly nearing completion. While the hook is held in a small vice the various pieces of tinsel and feather are neatly bound on. The tying silk is held taut while surplus pieces are trimmed off.*

at the eye, it is wound closely round the shank as far as the curve, and back again to form a second layer; the end is then held taut in a catch on the bench edge. As the only dressing of this fly is a hackle, a suitable black-dyed cock hackle feather is taken and the lower end trimmed off with scissors to leave a short length of bare quill. This is now attached to the fly body with three or four turns of silk, gripped delicately at the tip with the hackle pliers and wound round the body so that the fibres part to give a spidery appearance. It is tied again at the eye, the surplus silk cut off, and secured by a neat whip finish. Finally, a drop of clear varnish is applied with the dubbing needle to seal the silk, taking care not to fill the eye of the hook. Time taken – one minute. (With a whip finish, the end of the silk is held under three turns, pulled tight and cut off; a neat method that is quicker done than described.)

By way of contrast, the Jock Scott is a salmon fly of considerable eye-appeal and difficulty in making; it can be tied on various sizes of hook. Black tying silk is used and, after waxing, wound almost to the curve of the hook. Here the rearmost section, the *tag* which all salmon flies have,

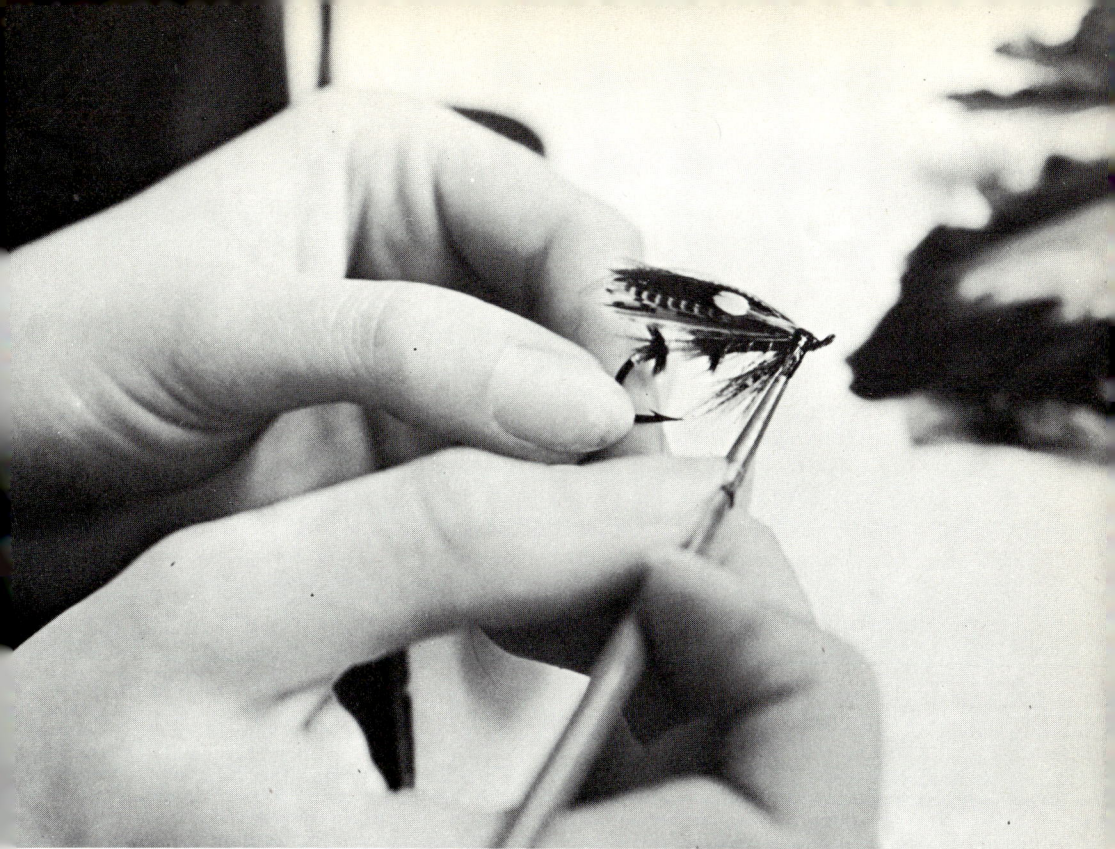

*The last step in making the Jock Scott is to secure the silk at the head by varnishing. Twenty-eight various materials have gone into this tiny creation about an inch long.*

is worked, in this case two turns of size 14 silver tinsel and two of yellow silk. Above this is attached the *tail*, a few fibres of golden pheasant crest. Forward of the tag comes the *butt*, a single black ostrich feather fibre, or *herl*, wound so that the tiny fibres, or *flue*, stand up. The main part of the body is in two halves, separated by another ostrich butt. The rear one is wound with yellow silk floss ribbed with three turns of size 15 silver tinsel; above and below it are attached yellow toucan feathers. The front half is wound with black silk floss ribbed with three turns of size 16 silver tinsel, under which is tied a black cock hackle. In front is another hackle of speckled guinea fowl.

The wings are equally complicated, consisting of, first, two largish pieces of white-tipped dark-mottled turkey tail feather tied to the top of the shank; they must be naturally left-hand and right-hand pieces in order to lie correctly. Next is tied in on each side a *mixed sheath* consisting of two fibres each of yellow, scarlet and blue swan, speckled bustard, florican bustard and golden pheasant tail. By stroking together the strands, the barbules engage as in a natural feather, and they must, of course, all be from the same feather side to marry properly. Over this sheath are two strands of peacock sword tail feather, and then another married section of two pieces each of teal and summer duck, followed by strips of mallard to give a dark outline to the 'wings'. Each section so carefully attached overlaps, rather like weather-boarding, but does not obscure the one below; the apex is a *topping* of golden pheasant crest. Partly overlapping the sides of the 'wings' are jungle cock feathers, whose natural golden 'eyes' give the fly some resemblance to a minnow, and small pieces of kingfisher. All these items must be tied firmly, yet delicately, so there is no undue build-up of material at the head; this is finally tied off and given two coats of varnish, first brown, then black. No fewer than twenty-eight different materials go into the making of this one fly, all on a hook which may be less than an inch long. Time taken – twenty-five minutes. The Jock Scott is regarded as one of the classic salmon flies and its tying such a test of skill that enthusiasts look on it as a thing of beauty.

A word ought to be said at this point regarding the names given to fishing flies, since they have a significance which is doubtless lost to non-sportsmen. Some trout flies have names referring to the insects they are derived from, such as the Black Gnat and Stone Fly, others refer to the materials used in their making, such as the Bustard and Red and the Jungle Cock. Names of clubs and lodges are preserved in flies like the Houghton Ruby and the Mar Lodge, and of fishermen and keepers in many others. Jock Scott was a keeper on the River Tweed for Lord John Scott in 1850, and Lunn's Particular is a memorial to a famous keeper of the Houghton Club of Stockbridge. In a number of instances the colours have suggested the name, for example the Blue Upright and the Cardinal, but more than a few must be creations of fancy. There is surely an anglers' pantomime waiting to be written about the affair between Reckless William and Hairy Mary and their adventures in escaping from the clutches of Killer Jock and the Black Doctor, before being rescued by the Silver Fairy with the Coachman who brings them safely to the Parson . . .

It is perhaps rather surprising that Miss Wakeford, whose work so obviously suits her natural dexterity and temperament, should have taken it up almost by accident. She and her father both fish, and when some years ago he gave her a fly-dressing kit in the hope of a mutually beneficial return, it was the beginning of a new interest. She had the foresight, more-over, to see that it might have commercial possibilities, and set herself to study and practise the craft. After many frustrations and a good deal of advertising, she at length realised those possibilities and now sends her work by post to all parts of Britain and even to North America; not the least remarkable part of that achievement being that all her sales are to private customers. Today, Miss Wakeford's skill is widely known, her little workshop is a place of resort for anglers on the Test and Itchen, and she is in some demand as a tutor for fly-tying classes. Izaak Walton would have approved of that, for he was one who knew the value of sound instruction: 'I confess, no direction can be given to make a man of a dull capacity able to make a Flie well; and yet I know, this with a little practice will help an ingenuous Angler in a good degree: but to see a Flie made by an Artist in that kind, is the best teaching to make it . . .'

# The polo stick maker

It was in the 1850s that a certain Captain Sherer, otherwise unknown, organised the first recorded game of polo among British army officers in Assam and so fired the enthusiasm for a game which later spread to most of the horse-using countries of the world. The game is actually very ancient and probably originated in Persia, whence it spread across Asia, and was found surviving in the nineteenth century in remote parts of the northeast and northwest frontiers of India. Its name is derived from the Tibetan dialect word for the willow, *pulu*, from whose roots the balls are made. (Bamboo root is also used.)

The need to have one's own highly-trained pony and access to a pitch 300 yds × 200 yds always tended to restrict the sport to the well-to-do and it was especially popular among commissioned ranks of the army in India; this helps to explain why one of the two firms in England making polo sticks is located at Aldershot, in the traditional heart of British army territory.

When the firm was founded, nearly ninety years ago, there was sufficient demand to support several others, and up to the Second World War the Aldershot firm needed four craftsmen. Raymond Turner, who joined the firm from school during the War, now has just one young trainee, so the craft has become a distinctly uncommon one. Fortunately for business, polo sticks have a hard and somewhat short life and during the summer months Mr Turner's workshop may be kept busy until 10 o'clock in the evening, meeting the orders and carrying out repairs. They make the balls too, while the shop downstairs stocks a remarkable range of all the other things that polo enthusiasts need for themselves and their ponies.

For those who have never examined one at close quarters, a polo stick is very much like a long-handled mallet. Its head is cylindrical, about 9 in long, and usually weighs 6-8 oz; the cane, stiff or whippy as preferred, terminates in a covered handgrip. The length of a polo stick is related to the height of the mount being ridden and may vary from 44 in, for a pony

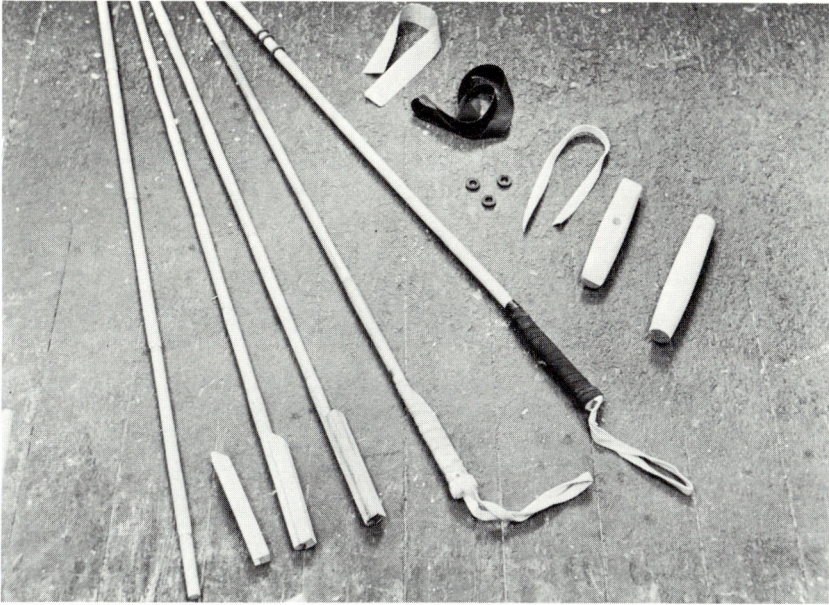

*Stages in making a polo stick, with finished and unfinished heads. The small rubber rings which go on just above the head serve to cushion mis-strikes.*

of 13.2 hands, to 52 in for 15.2 hands, though the user's preference plays a part; so may style of riding, which accounts for the very short sticks of 38 in which Mr Turner supplies to Saudi Arabian players. A polo ball is struck not with the end but the side of the head, and to avoid digging in the turf it is tapered or trimmed in a choice of styles. The head is attached to the cane at a slight angle to compensate for swinging it clear of the pony's flank.

The versatile bamboo provides the chief material for most polo sticks, with ash, sycamore, and sometimes mulberry, also being used for heads. Painted bamboo keeps out the damp, while when covered with vellum it resists fraying and stands up better to service in dry climates. Only solid root can be used for heads. Mr Turner gets them supplied rough-turned and likes to let them season for three years before use – a wise precaution in any case, as by that time a good many have been made useless by dormant insect attack. Shaping is done on a mechanical belt sander, followed by drilling for the cane and painting of any club colours which may be required. Cane for handles comes in bundles up to 9 ft long, and once more a lot of wastage has to be tolerated. Mr Turner needs it $\frac{5}{8}$-$\frac{3}{4}$ in thick, allowing for taper to the head end, and fairly close-jointed for strength.

*An old treadle lathe has been adapted to turn the sticks and make a neat job when the head ends are being glued and bound.*

The cane, too, has to be seasoned and where necessary straightened in a rubber-faced clamp, after softening in a box of hot sand. Joints are trimmed with a knife and smoothed down with the sander.

To make the handgrip, a shaped wooden block is glued to the thicker end of the cane and bound first with broad canvas strip, then with cotton, towelling or rubber tape, incorporating a strong wrist loop. The head end of the cane is whipped with linen thread over cotton tape and sized with glue before being glued and wedged into the head. Three rubber rings are slipped onto the cane at this end to afford some protection from the ball in case of mis-strikes. An old treadle lathe has been ingeniously adapted by Mr Turner to speed up the whipping operation – by rotating the cane between the widely-spaced head- and tail-stocks and holding the thread against it, a firm, neat winding is quickly made. Finally the handle is rubbed over with linseed oil.

Aldershot-made polo sticks go all over the world, wherever the game is played, along with accessories as diverse as chukka clocks and knee protectors: everything, in fact, that players and their mounts require.

94

*Maker and product. Behind him are shelves full of rough-turned heads made from bamboo root, ash and sycamore.*

# The saddler

If the horse's health depends to a great extent upon the skills of the vet and the farrier, its efficiency as a working animal owes much to the saddler; and when one considers how for thousands of years, until well within living memory, the horse was a critical factor in transport and communications, the saddler's part should not be underrated. He was one of the key craftsmen of the self-supporting rural community, along with those other stalwarts the blacksmith and the carpenter. In smaller places, he probably undertook all the leatherwork not actually done by the cobbler, and sometimes even the shoe repairs as well. In the towns, saddlery and harness making were regarded as two distinct occupations, and the craftsmen were further sub-divided into *brown saddlers* making equipment for riding horses, and those making equipment for draught or working horses, the *black saddlers*; the latter often worked as journeymen travelling round to farms. Black saddles and harness were favoured for working purposes because they could receive regular oiling to keep out the wet. Few people today can remember the way in which a good set of harness enhanced a stylishly turned-out pair, assisted by the smart plated fittings and accessories chosen from the makers' catalogues.

When the internal combustion engine began to replace the horse on the roads, the volume of work decreased rapidly and saddlery and harness making came together. During the Second World War, however, when agriculture was expanded on an unprecedented scale and many farms were still without tractors, saddlers were at a premium and the trade enjoyed a boom. But the decline could only be checked, and not until recent times does it appear to have been halted.

The reason for this is to be seen in the way that riding for pleasure has restored an interest in the horse that has all-but disappeared from farming (except for one or two farmers who keep a few for old times' sake). An Alresford saddler, Jim Hounsom says: 'A lot of people are under the impression that this is a dying trade, but the people in it are dying quicker

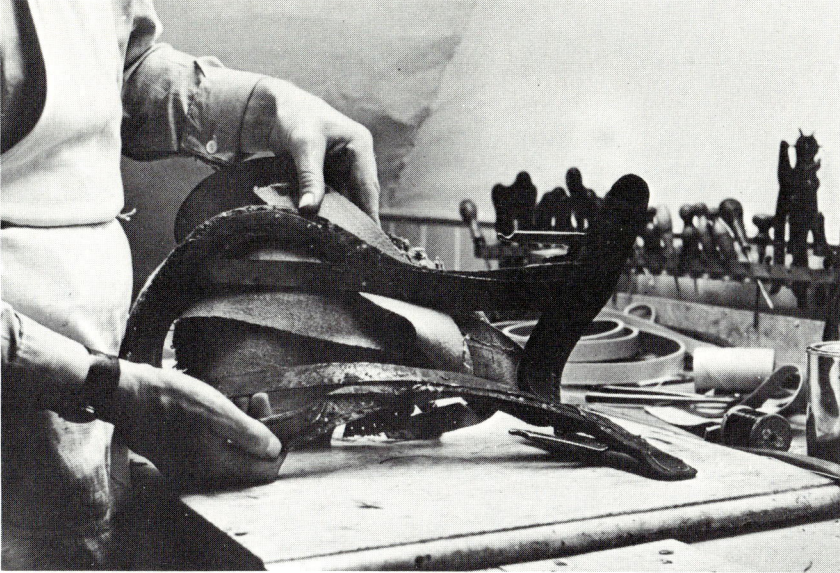

*A saddler is often called on to rebuild a saddle, and that means stripping it right down to the foundation or saddle tree. To the right are the points, and projecting backwards from them the stirrup bars.*

than the trade.' There is an unhappy ring of truth in his words, for even while this chapter was in the making the services of two local saddlers were lost, one by death, the other by retirement; the numbers still working are small. These days, virtually all production of new saddles is concentrated in Walsall, with a number of cheap ones being imported from India, and making them by hand in small quantities is quite uneconomic. Thus, although qualified to make saddles right through, Mr Hounsom concentrates on repair work and this often involves a complete reconstruction demanding all his skill.

He was born in Sussex and it was the influence of a friend that led him to seek work with a firm of saddlers in Lewes when he left school. He liked the work, and when the time came for National Service he was posted to the Household Cavalry, in which regiment he stayed for six years and completed his saddler's training. Returning to civilian life, he spent some twelve years as an improver with a well-known Hampshire saddler and was then appointed manager of his present business. This was set up a few years ago with the primary aim of selling American 'Western' style saddles and proved so successful that English saddlery and a wide range of related goods were added.

The import of Western saddlery is a riding phenomenon of our times

*A number of specialised tools are employed in saddlery, the half-moon knife and its smaller relation the head knife being in frequent use for cutting jobs.*

that is meeting with increasing success, and not just because of its associations or elaborate decoration. The Western saddle has a high front and rear and is ridden long-legged; this keeps the rider securely seated with a tall pommel to hang on to for extra confidence. With this kind of saddle, the inexperienced can make a reasonable attempt to enjoy the pleasures of riding, and, what is more, it has been found that physically handicapped youngsters are able to enter into a compensatory activity of some therapeutic value. There's no sliding off if the pony bends down to crop!

The skill of the saddler lies in making a piece of equipment that will enable the horse to carry the burden of a correctly distributed weight, and his prime consideration must be for the comfort of the horse. This involves not only correct construction of the saddle, but also ensuring that there are no projections, rough edges or stitching that will cause irritation. The basic foundation of a general-purpose saddle is the *saddle-tree*, a light U-shaped framework of laminated beech which lies along the horse's back. The base of the U is curved over the spine, and the ends joined by another arched section which extends a little down either side over the withers. These are the *points*, which help to support the stirrup bar. Steel plates reinforce the tree, and flat steel springs run its length on the inside. If

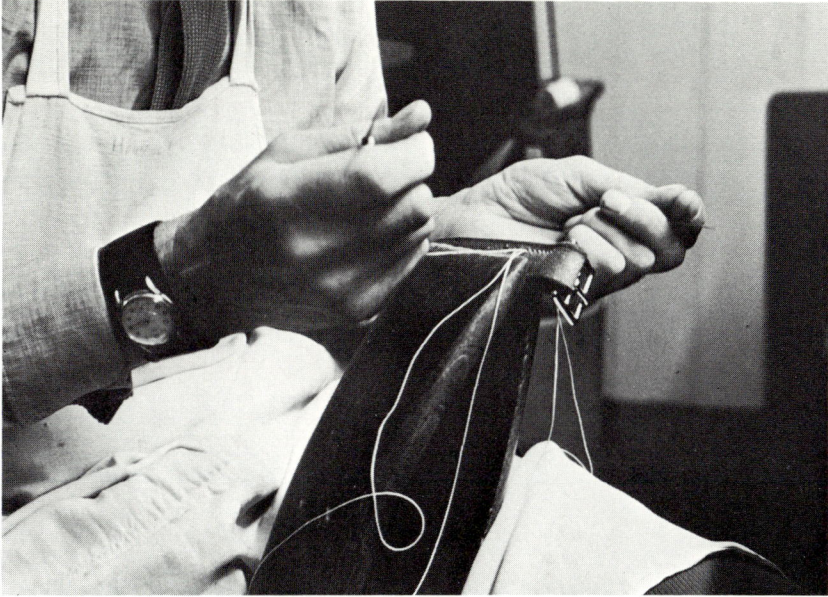

*With the leather firmly gripped in the clams, a long wooden vice held between the knees, the hands are left free for sewing with two needles from both sides of the work.*

Mr Hounsom is called on to rebuild a saddle, he may have to strip it right down to the tree and begin by mending it with additional metal plates, glued and bound with linen. Under the tree, and again carefully shaped to avoid any pressure on the spine, are fastened the *panels*, thick pads covered in thin, supple panel hide for best saddles, linen or serge for cheaper ones. The panels are stuffed with grey wool, or sometimes felt or polystyrene foam, using a *seat iron* like a long bent screwdriver with a notched end to insert the wool: a job that calls for some skill. To allow the right depth of seat to be built on the saddle, webs are fastened between the front and rear arches of the tree. They are put on wet, stretched with a *web strainer*, which is similar to a pair of pliers with a lever on the side, and tacked in place with a light *saddle hammer*. Such is the force of tradition that, instead of using non-rusting nails, blue cut tacks are used, with a strip of leather placed over the webs to minimise rust damage! As the webs dry they become taut.

Above the saddle-tree come first the *flaps* of hogskin-grained cowhide, then the *skirts*, large thick panels of the same hide which take the wear over the stirrup bars, and finally the *seat*. This is made of pigskin and is stuffed with white wool – the rider's comfort is at last becoming a con-

*Some of the wide range of tools used by the saddler.*

*Left to right, top row. Scriber: marks guideline for stitching. Keyhole punch: makes slots for stud fastenings. Pricking irons: position stitch holes. Wad punch. Oval punch. Round punches. Crew or buckle punches: cut hole for buckle tongues.*

*Left to right, bottom row. Screw crease: used as the scriber. Callipers. Half-moon knife. Head knife. Trimming knife. Awls.*

sideration. Any, or all, of these parts may need repair or replacement, and upon their correct attachment, fit and proportion one saddler will judge the work of another; he will also look for neatness of stitching – of which more later. Mr Hounsom does not like to sell a saddle 'off the peg' but prefers to take it to the horse and adjust or change it until both horse and rider are satisfied.

At the heart of the saddler's work lies skill in leatherwork. In former times, an apprentice – who probably had to clean his master's boots, open up the shop and act as general factotum – spent his first year learning nothing more than how to make threads and sew even stitches; he was certainly not allowed to touch work for a customer. Now that the period of apprenticeship is down to four years (encouraged by concentrated courses run by the Worshipful Company of Saddlers) Mr Hounsom's lads spend a shorter time at this stage and then follow a progressive training programme. But good, even stitching is still regarded as a hallmark of the skilled saddler.

Ready-made thread is mostly used these days but it is still necessary to make up heavy-gauge thread for some jobs. Single-strand hemp thread is drawn out to an appropriate length and doubled up as often as required. Then it is pulled taut against a hook on the workshop bench and well rubbed with a lump of beeswax; it is from this action that the saddler gets his army nickname of 'Waxy'. Arranging the threads so their ends do not all come together, the saddler rolls them on his thigh and produces a long, tapering point that will pass easily through the needle's eye. To ensure a perfectly straight line of stitches, a guideline is first made, parallel to the edge of the leather, by lightly drawing along it a pair of callipers or a simple wooden scriber with fixed points, and on this line a *pricking iron* is tapped with a mallet to leave regular slanting marks spaced from five to sixteen to the inch. These are pierced with a diamond-section awl of selected size, and by doing this, all the stitches will lie evenly. By using waxed thread somewhat thicker than the needle, the hole is well plugged and the stitches will still hold even if the tops are worn off. To minimise such wear the stitches are pulled a little into the leather, which therefore takes the rubbing. When sewing two pieces of leather together the saddler uses a pair of needles, stitching from each side alternately and holding the work in the jaws of his *clams*, a long, springy wooden vice steadied between his knees. He uses both straight and curved needles of various gauges and has his own special method of threading them so the thread cannot pull out; thread is selected to match the metal fittings – yellow, white or black.

Mr Hounsom needs various other tools for his work. His *half-round* (or *half-moon*) *knife*, that looks like an old-fashioned kitchen herb chopper, could well be the saddler's trademark for it is used for all rough cutting-out of leather and for cutting long pieces. A smaller version, the *head knife*, is used for detailed work. A *plough gauge* will cut strips up to about 6 in wide and is chiefly used for making straps. To remove rough edges on newly cut leather that might chafe horse or rider, an *edge tool*, rather like a notched gouge is used, and a larger version, the *skirt shave*, is used on the edges of saddle skirts. A *splitting machine* fastened to the bench top can be used to reduce the thickness of leather. Stirrup bars sometimes have to be riveted on, calling for an 8 oz hammer to be used with a short piece of old railway line as an anvil. *Riveting sets* are used to draw up and round off other rivets. A whole range of punches is needed; *wad punches; round*

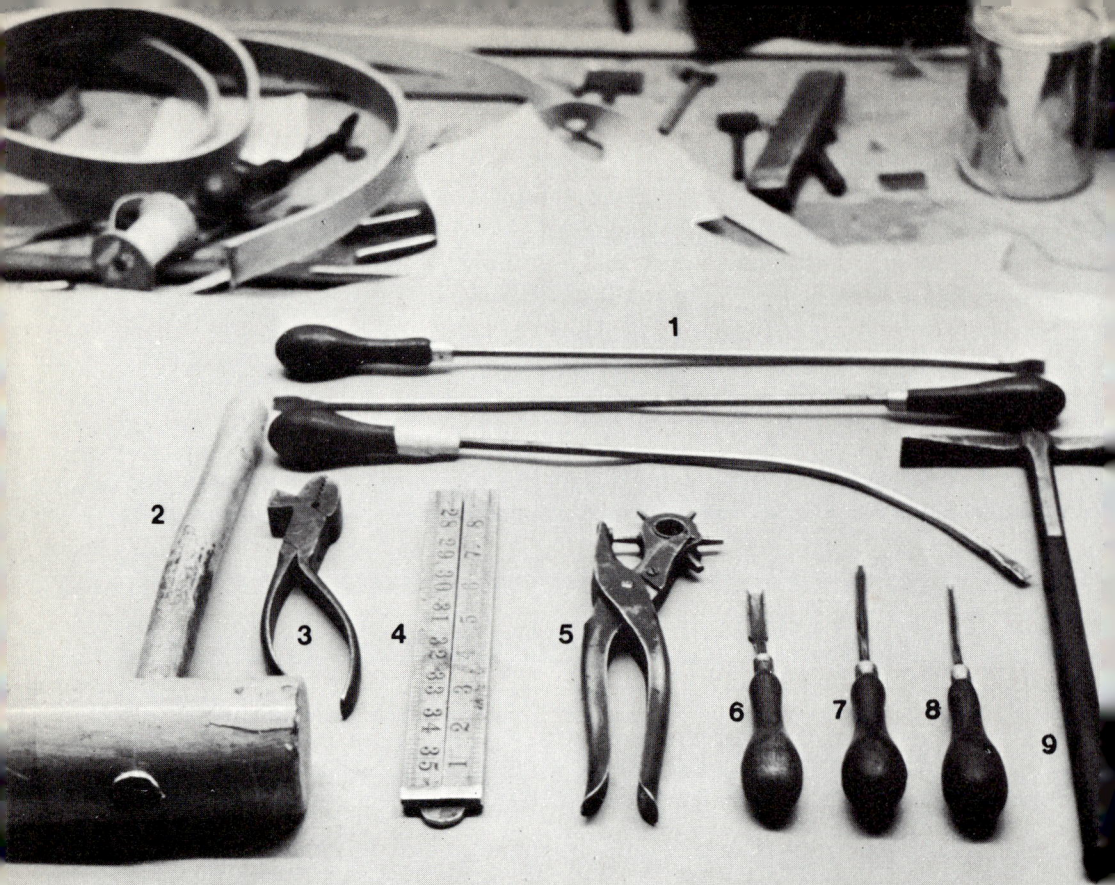

*(1) Seat irons: insert saddle stuffing (2) Mallet: used with punches (3) Web strainer: pulls seat webbing taut when nailing (4) Folding rule (5) Revolving eyelet punch (6-8) Edge tools: remove rough leather edges (9) Saddle hammer.*

*punches; oval* or *crew punches* used to cut the holes for large buckle tongues; a revolving *eyelet punch* and a *keyhole punch* to make slots or stud fastenings. To mark a neat parallel line on the edge of finished leatherwork a warm *creasing iron* with spade-shaped head is employed, and the same tool used hot over a stencil can be used for decoration. Mr Hounsom has two sewing machines but regards them as a necessary evil; they are all right for light jobs but as they only make a chain stitch, parts tend to separate with wear.

One of the interesting things arising from conversation with Mr Hounsom is his attitude to the economics of craftsmanship, an issue on which older generations often had only the haziest of notions. He sees that there must be a proper understanding of the relationship between time, overheads and prices if a craft is to survive and remain reasonably profitable, and that means concentrating on his proper skills and cutting down drastically on things like briefcase and handbag repairs, which are nothing to do with the real business of saddlery. Indeed, he believes that a business-like approach is vital for the survival of the craft, otherwise the saddler could well be, in his engaging metaphor, 'the Cinderella of the horse world'. Happily, riding remains a popular recreation and even with an improver and two apprentices Jim Hounsom can barely keep pace with all the saddle work coming in.

# The sailmaker

When Bert Clark's father started work in 1901, the first thing a sailmaker had to do was to make himself a pair of cotton over-trousers from 2½ yards of material supplied by his employer. Today, a sailmaker still wears the over-trousers but they are given to him ready-made, along with a pair of soft canvas shoes; the one to protect his own trousers when working on the floor of the *sail loft*, the other to prevent outside grit from being trodden into it. The change is symptomatic of the way sailmaking has altered over the last half-century – from making heavy sails in cotton and canvas by hand, many of them for large sailing vessels, to producing machine-sewn sails in light synthetics for small boat owners. The trade is full of tradition but continually experimenting and advancing under competitive pressures; virtually all production is for the leisure market, with only occasionally the excitement of making a new *suit* of sails for one of the large training schooners.

Mr Clark has lived in Gosport all his life and claims that he was 'more or less born on the water', and introduced to sailing before he was a month old. His grandfather was Captain of the famous floating bridge that ceased work in 1959 after 120 years' service, his father was a chargehand-sailmaker. When he was fourteen, Bert began a five-year apprenticeship in the same firm as his father, but it was not until he had spent a couple of years doing odd jobs as a 'lackey for the sailmakers' that he became a *bench hand* and started learning to sew.

Being keen and quick to learn, Mr Clark's prospects and his wages were good when he had completed his time. He had the job at his fingertips and there were plenty of opportunities for studying the functions of sail at first hand: he and a friend built their own boat, buying a plank a week out of their pocket money. In 1938, his sailing took a more serious turn and he began to train with the Auxiliary Company of HMS *Vernon*, carrying out 'Saturday afternoon minesweeping' in local waters. Soon it was the real thing and the quiet life of a *stab-rag* (Navy slang) was put aside until the War was over. The firm for which he now works was founded in the early 1970s, when the old-established one which he had joined as a boy decided to concentrate production elsewhere. This provided an opportunity for two young designers, one of boats, the other of sails, to set up a new service, designing and making sails for discriminating yachtsmen, and Mr Clark was asked to become Foreman Sailmaker. Now he supervises a team of sailmakers that at certain times of the year works far into the evening to keep up with an ever-increasing demand.

In his quest for sails that will be of maximum efficiency on the boat for which they are intended (meaning, in practice, that they will drive it faster than the next man's), the designer seeks the best setting sail with optimum curvature. In the case of a *spinnaker*, this will be a bag which fills with wind and pulls the boat forward; in the case of *fore-and-aft* sails (e.g., *mainsail* and *headsail*) he aims to create an aerofoil, rather like the wing of an aircraft. It is the negative pressure caused by wind acting upon the convex surface of a sail that produces three-quarters of its driving power, just as it produces lift for the aircraft. Thus, much care goes into the design and production of the right shape, bearing in mind its relation to the spill of wind from adjacent sails and the total achievement of the *rig*. The sail must set so there are no *girts*, or wrinkles, to upset the airflow as it spills smoothly off the rear edge, or *leech*, and to assist in keeping it flat, mainsails usually have horizontal pockets in the leech containing stiffening battens of wood or glass fibre.

The sail designer needs an intimate knowledge of the properties of sail-cloths. There is stretch in a panel of sailcloth cut across the bias but little along the thread line, and advantage can be taken of this to produce some of the *camber*, or fullness, by arranging the panels in various ways. At the same time, the designer has to remember the stresses to which the sail will be subject. Some striking cuts such as the 'sunray', 'spider web' and 'star' are the outcome of such contriving and although the effect may be spectacular if cloths of two colours are used, much seaming and wasteful cutting makes them expensive. Most of a sail's shape is built in by cutting the edges to a curve (*roach*) which makes fullness when they are hauled taut. Introducing extra width into tapered seams (making *broad seams*) can also contribute, as well as counteracting localised strain in the sail. For most work Mr Clark's firm uses a Terylene sailcloth specially woven in weights from 3 oz to 24 oz a square yard. For spinnakers and drifting sails a light-weight nylon of $\frac{3}{4}$ oz a square yard, is used. The most-used widths are 21 in and 33 in, narrow cloths being popular for racing as more seams make for greater strength. Canvas and cotton are now quite uncommon.

Such is the popularity of sailing that many firms are manufacturing sails on a mass-production basis and it is these sails that the purchaser of

*Sailmaking requires plenty of space. Here, using a spleen stick held by prickers, the roach which will give fullness to the sail is being marked out. Permanent lines on the floor are used when making up standard-size sails.*

an inexpensive ready-rigged boat is likely to acquire. But the more discerning yachtsman, going in for racing or long-distance cruising, demands something better and needs the services of a sail designer. With him he can discuss the boat and its proposed use, and any personal preferences; and the designer can apply his formulae and suggest cloth weights and fittings that will give the best service. A typical suit of sails for an enthusiast may consist of a mainsail, four headsails and three spinnakers, giving plenty of choice for different conditions.

In the case of a sail of standard design, the cloths are cut out on a bench according to long paper patterns or other patterns permanently drawn on the sail loft floor. For special sails the outline must be chalked on the floor or marked out with white twine stretched round wood-handled *prickers*. It needs plenty of space and Mr Clark does not find the loft too large at 150 ft long by 44 ft wide. Various areas are set aside for different kinds of work; for example, the *spreading floor*, the *bench floor*, and the *machine floor*. The loft is well lit by large windows from which there are views of busy boatyards and the panorama of Portsmouth harbour, with the reproach of HMS *Victory*'s bare masts rising on the further shore.

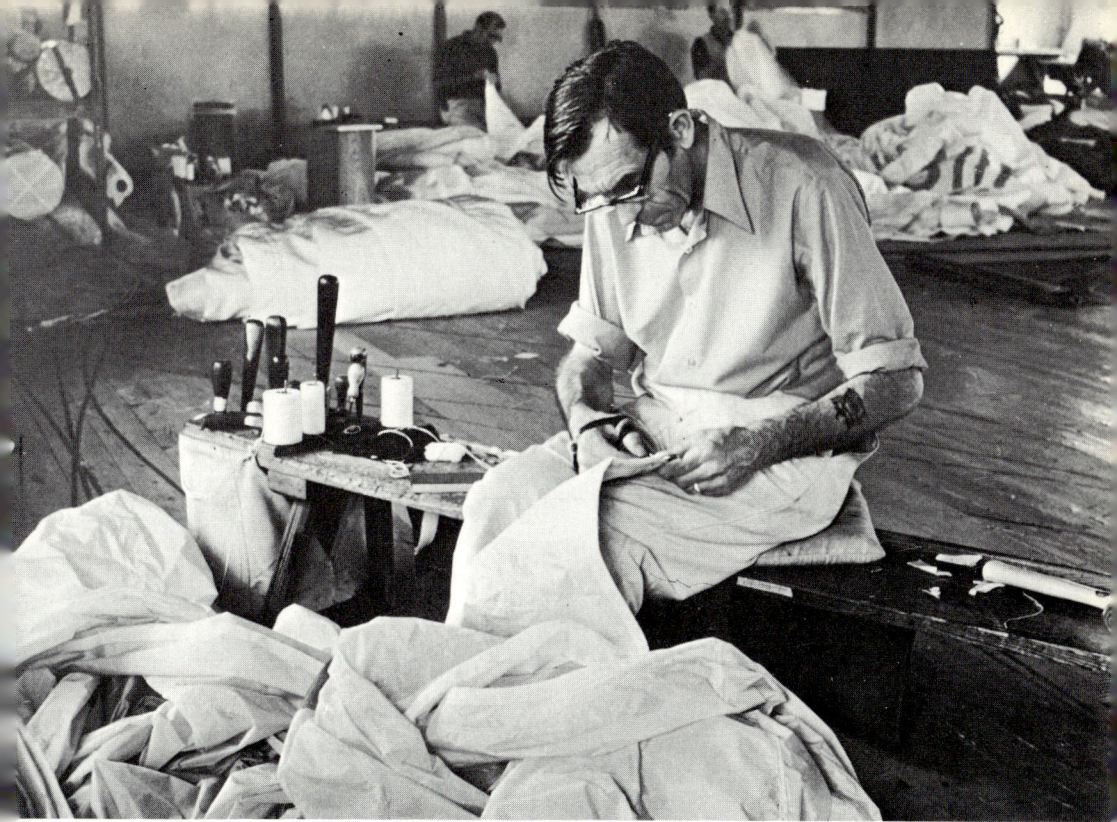

*Sitting on his bench, the sailmaker has his tools conveniently to hand on his right. A head bag round the end of the bench prevents sails being snagged on their points. Tools, bench and white cotton over-trousers are all traditional.*

After careful inspection for faults, the cloth is cut from the roll and laid in lengths side by side under the string outline, allowing up to 4 in clearance round the edges for the *tablings* or seams. A sailmaker scorns the use of scissors for this or any other operation: they have no place in his kit. Instead, a *bench knife* serves for all cutting purposes, kept razor sharp on an emery board which is leather-backed for fine stropping. By drawing the tip of the blade between two warp threads, a guide is made when cutting a cloth at right-angles to the selvedge. However, synthetic cloths are not always amenable to this method and as they tend to pucker when cutting (and perhaps because the women machinists help with cutting out) scissors are now allowed on lightweight cloths. The laid cloths overlap ($\frac{1}{2}$ in to $1\frac{1}{4}$ in according to weight) to the coloured thread which runs along the selvedge and a pencil *hooking mark* is made across the overlap about every 9 in. This enables the two cloths to be kept level when sewing, as there is a tendency for the bottom one to creep. It derives from use of the *bench hook* attached to the sailmaker's bench but is useful to machinists too. Before the cloths are seamed up, the boat's racing numbers are positioned on opposite sides of two adjacent cloths and held temporarily by stapling before being machined on; it is much easier to turn a single cloth round under the machine than a whole sail!

Everything about the bench on which the sailmaker sits to do most of his work is prescribed by custom. The top is a plank 7 ft 6 in long by 1 ft wide, supported on legs 1 ft 3 in high. Along the back is a lip to stop tools falling off and in front of it runs a groove for small items such as needles. The end to the user's right is perforated with a square arrangement of holes in which tools are kept, points downwards, and around them is tacked a canvas *head bag* to prevent sails being torn or snagged on them. On the front edge of the bench, close to the tools, the bench hook is attached by a length of cord; it allows the sailmaker to strain his cloths across his knees as he sews. Two square canvas bags are attached to the back of the bench, that nearest to the tools for stowing oddments such as twine and *housewife* (needle roll), the other for the sailmaker's *tommy* (lunch). The men no longer eat a 9 o'clock lunch at their benches as they did when Mr Clark was young, but custom decrees that the bag remains. In former times many sailmakers chewed tobacco (no smoking is allowed in sail lofts) and used the head bag, into which they had gathered the oakum produced by trimming and splicing ropes, as a convenient spittoon. Snuff-taking was also common.

Sailmakers' needles are triangular in section and come in a range of sizes from 0 (large) to 19 (small). The three largest are large indeed and are used with heavy twine for big roping jobs, as described later. Today's synthetic ropes are a good deal smaller than hemp and are sewn with lighter twine, so the big needles now have more curiosity value than use.

The most-used stitch is a *seaming stitch* which goes on and off the edge when joining overlapping cloths. Both edges can be sewn from one side, thanks to the selvedge thread acting as a guide. A *round seaming stitch* is used when joining two adjacent edges; a *cross stitch* or a *herringbone stitch* is used when repairing tears. The needle is threaded with about a yard of thread at a time, used double and rubbed with a block of beeswax to encourage cohesion of the strands; beeswax may also be used on the fingers when the needle chafes. No real sailmaker ever starts his work with a knot – the end is tucked under the seam and held tight by the first few stitches. In seaming work, a yard of thread makes 45 stitches and goes about 9 in, and the merit of such frequent stopping-off is that if a seam tears it is unlikely to part for any length. Using thread in a contrasting colour to the cloth makes damage easier to spot. Beginners' stitches that are too far apart are sometimes known as *dog's teeth* or *homeward bound stitches* (also applied to emergency repairs).

As he sews, the sailmaker presses down his seam from time to time with a square steel tool called a *rubber*. Stitching will not bed into synthetics

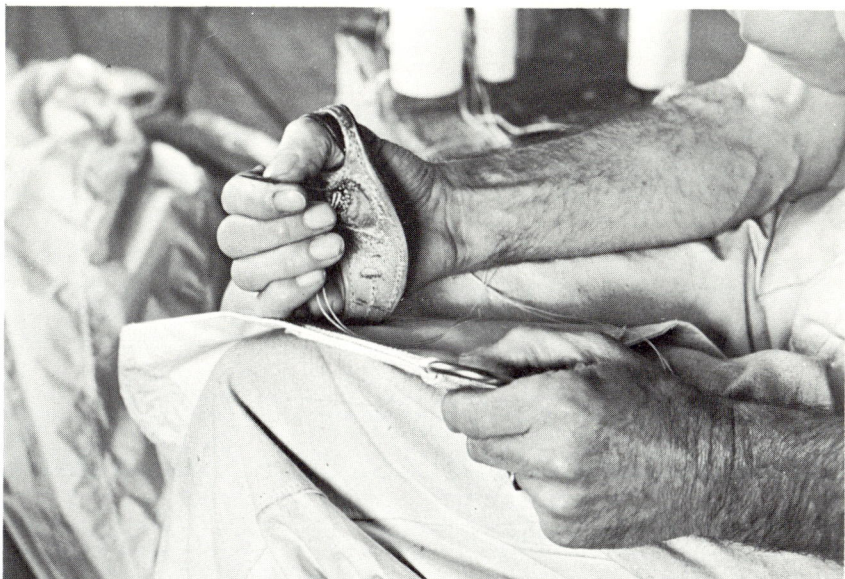

*Heavier sails are still sewn by hand, a task which would be impossible without the seaming palm to push the needle through the cloth – there may be a dozen layers at reinforcement points.*

as it does into cotton, but good hand work still lies flatter than machining and is consequently less prone to chafing and failure. The initial cost is much greater but the experienced sailor knows its worth. Cloths over 15 oz weight are always hand sewn, as machines cannot cope with the heavy thread needed. Whether hand- or machine-sewn, a seam of even width is most important to avoid hard spots and wrinkles when the sail is in use.

The *seaming palm* could be described as the sailmaker's best friend. It is a kind of leather loop which goes round his hand, having a hole in it for the thumb and a pitted metal needle guard set over the ball of the thumb. Wearing it, he can exert considerable pressure on the end of the needle when sewing. A variation, the *roping palm*, is used for heavy work like sewing a rope on the tabling of a sail; it has fewer pits in the guard for larger needles, and there is a built-up collar round the thumb to help in pulling the stitches through.

Some types of sail are made in two or more main parts, of which the *mitre-cut* sail is a common example; here, two groups of cloths meet at an angle. When the two parts are made up they are laid out on the spreading floor to be aligned along the mitre, or *last*, before being sewn up. Then the sail is spread again for the edges to be shaped. Long, thin wooden battens known as *spleen sticks* are positioned on the sail with prickers and the roach

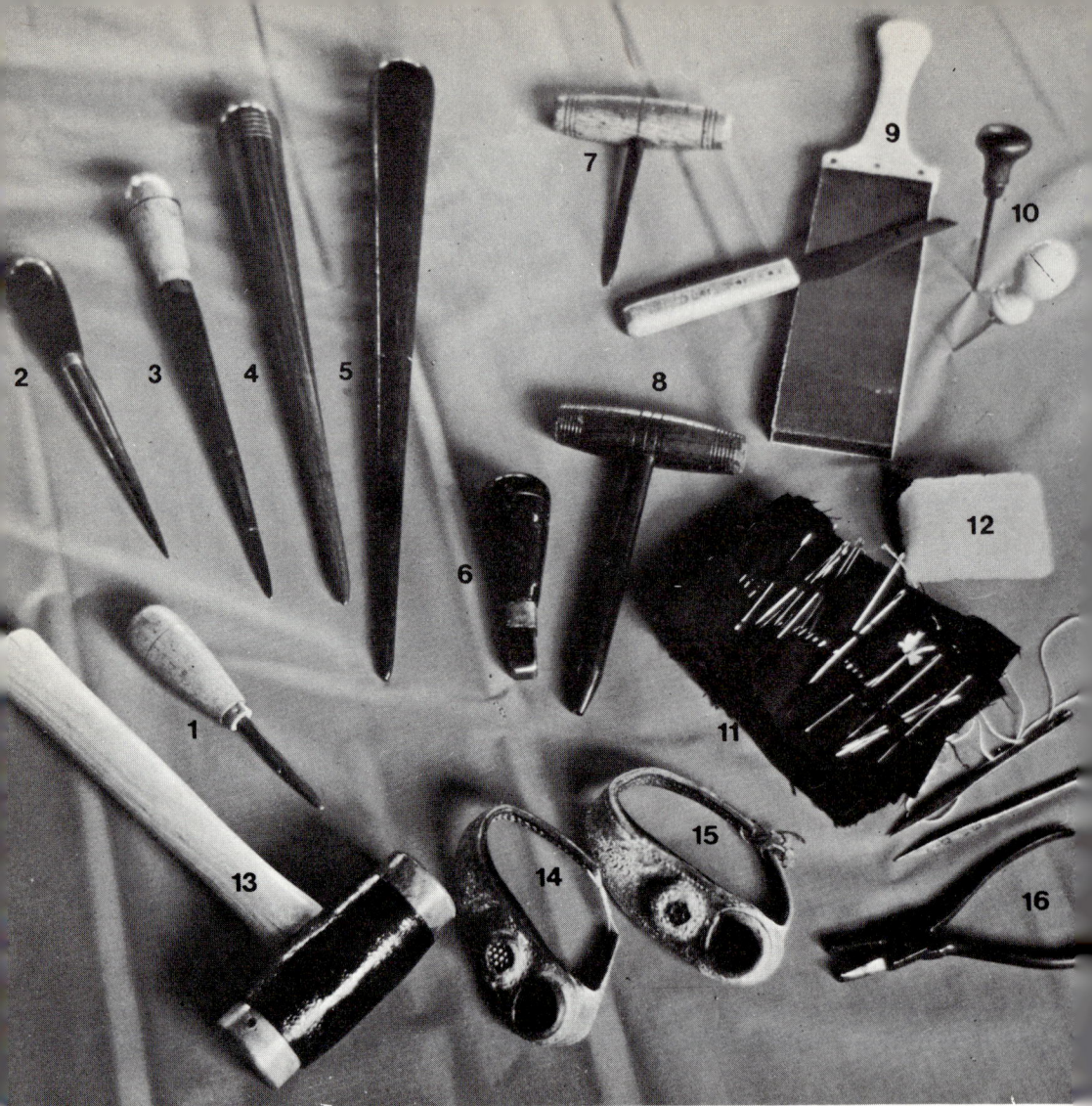

The sailmaker's toolkit.

*(1-3) Spikes: open the strands when splicing wire rope (4-5) Fids: used in splicing rope and when stitching an eye (6) Rubber: smoothes stitching (7-8) Stitch mallets: push needles, pull threads (9) Bench knife and emery board (10) Prickers: hold sail cloths when being spread (11) Housewife and needles (12) Beeswax (13) Mallet: used with punches when cutting holes and attaching eyelets (14) Seaming palm: used for most sewing work (15) Roping palm: used for roping and heavy sewing (16) Pliers.*

curves drawn off by pencil. Using the back of his knife the sailmaker *rubs in* the edges, turning them back on the guidelines, and trims off the surplus. While spread, the positions for the reinforcing patches are marked on the sail; great attention is paid to strengthening sails at their points of greatest stress, the corners, where there may be as many as fourteen layers of cloth.

Going back to the bench, the patches, tablings and batten pockets are sewn and the *head*, *clew* and *tack* corner eyes sewn in. The eyes are in two parts: a ring which is first sewn on after a hole has been cut, and a turnover which is pressed in to protect the stitching. To minimise the number of stitch holes round the ring the thread may be used in four, or even six parts. A lignum vitae *fid*, a spike between 10 and 18 in long, is used to press the stitches smooth inside the ring (it is also used to open the strands when splicing rope; a similar *spike* with a steel shaft is used on wire rope). Small eyelets, for the attachment of mainsail slides are worked in the same way, although they may be attached by punches in the case of small boat sails, a hole being first made with a circular cutter. This used to be done on a block of lead, but experience has shown that it is simpler to work on the end of an elm block, sawing a section off when it gets worn. Grey chromed leather is sewn over some of the metal fittings on the sail as a protection against wet.

By this stage, *roping* of the sail can be carried out: the attachment of ropes for further strength along the luff and foot. As with other plain sewing jobs, this can be done by machine in the case of light ropes, and actually has the advantage of even tension, but hand sewing is stronger, although difficult to do well; a man who can do good roping is highly valued in any loft. The rope is marked with a pencil line along its length and the edge of the sail is kept level to it, sewing between the strands with a round stitch. A dulled needle is easier for this job than a sharp one. Roping is sometimes hard work: Mr Clark recounts the effort required to sew up a heavy mainsail rope with a steel core in each strand, each stitch taking a full minute to make. In tough work like this, the *stitch mallet* comes in handy. It is like an old-fashioned carriage key and has a seven-sided steel shaft round which the sewing thread can be wound and then turned to pull it tight; a hollow in the tapered end of the shaft is useful for pushing through reluctant needles. One of the neat tricks in roping, is to make a tapered end to a rope by unravelling the strands and scraping each down, then twisting them together again. This avoids having an untidy end which might chafe.

One of the last operations on headsails is inserting the PVC-covered wire *fore-stay* in the tabling of the luff. To do this, the sail is stretched on a stay wire and marked every yard for the positioning of hand-sewn *seizings* which prevent the sail slipping on it; it is also seized at each end from the head and tack rings. Finally, every finished sail is carefully checked over by Mr Clark or the senior sailmaker and packed in its own bag marked with the sail name, serial number, boat name and racing number. A log of all sails is kept as a reference for future repairs or replacements.

# DESIGN CRAFTS

# The bookbinder

It is sometimes the case that a craftsman who is not catering for local needs is better known outside his area than within it. One such is Roger Powell, the bookbinder, whose work is admired in distant places by lovers and guardians of fine books. His workshop is on the ground floor of a former barn at Froxfield, built in the reign of George II. It is a large, airy room whose windows look out on to green lawns and a green lane and light up the natural matchboard lining of the walls. Built-in cupboards, benches and sinks support a scatter of tools and unfinished work and indicate a degree of planning not often met with in smaller workshops; more benches and large items like screw presses and a board chopper occupy the centre of the room. Mr Powell, who describes himself as an artist-craftsman, works here with his assistants in the relaxed atmosphere of those absorbed in an occupation that is creative, satisfying and un-hurried.

The workshop is only a mile or so from Bedales School, where Mr Powell grew up in the tradition of practical studies for which it is noted and where his father was Second Master. While at Bedales he learned the elements of bookbinding from his father and first met Douglas Cockerell whose work *Bookbinding and the Care of Books* was an important influence on him (another was Edward Johnston's *Writing, Illuminating and Lettering* with its illustrations of the Book of Kells). But it was to be a long time before Mr Powell thought of turning to the craft in order to make a living. The First World War followed hot upon his schooldays and when he returned from it as a qualified pilot he launched into a quite different kind of venture – poultry farming, in fact. After persevering with it for several years his old interest in bookbinding proved stronger and he went to study at the Central School of Arts and Crafts, London, eventually setting up his own workshop in 1931.

It proved hard, however, for a newcomer to establish himself, partly because clients were reluctant to entrust work to an unknown binder, and in desperation he wrote to Douglas Cockerell asking for suggestions. The outcome was an invitation to work for Douglas Cockerell and Son, which he did with such success that in 1936 he became a partner; the link was maintained until 1947 with Sydney Cockerell, after his father's death. Mr Powell looks back on those years as the most formative in his career, believing that he owes his own success as a binder largely to the support he received from that famous workshop.

Mr Powell is on record as saying that, 'A book is a three-dimensional articulated artefact,' a definition sounding strange only as long as we take the physical structure for granted while concentrating on the contents. Like many other things, the making of most books today is a matter of mass-production by sophisticated machinery and we accept the products as a matter of course. The trade binder produces cases to be attached – often inadequately – to machine-made assemblies of pages, whereas the studio binder sees a book as the sum of its parts, each contributing to a working mechanism. Much of his expertise lies in understanding the function and relationship of these parts. It is true that there are some binders for whom decoration of the cover is all important, and some collectors who would not put the binding to the test by opening the book, but they represent an unbalanced approach to the craft.

Much of Mr Powell's work is concerned with the re-binding of old books, both printed and manuscript, so ensuring their survival and safe use for posterity. When Florence suffered the disastrous floods of 1966, thousands of old and precious volumes were submerged for weeks in flood-water contaminated with mud and sewage. Local emergency treatment consisted of sponging off the worst dirt and drying them, but skilled treatment and re-binding were called for on a large scale, beyond what was available from Italian resources. So outside assistance was sought, and among many European binders Mr Powell's workshop was commissioned to help in tackling the huge problem of book conservation: a problem even vaster, possibly, than that posed by flooded paintings, sculptures, tapestries and other works of art. Mr Powell's workshop was responsible for the mending of about a thousand books and the complete washing, repair and re-binding of another hundred. Some idea of what this means can be gained from the following account of the basic processes of conservation and re-binding, bearing in mind that the binder must be prepared to meet with many variations in materials and construction.

After the book has been checked and found complete, it is first *pulled*, that is, taken apart to separate the folded sections and remove old sewing threads and glue. Stained leaves must be washed, while others which have become soft with age may have to be re-sized in a weak gelatine solution to bond the fibres. Leaves that have been damaged are repaired by pasting

*An old volume may require a good deal of conservation work before re-binding can begin. In this instance, one of the badly-cockled vellum leaves of a manuscript is being stretched out to dry after damping.*

on slightly oversized patches of Japanese tissue torn to shape, so that the long fibres present no visible join. A similar technique is used in repairing vellum leaves, the overlapping edges being first scarfed with a glasspaper stick to reduce thickness and disguise the join. Repairs are pressed firmly between sheets of blotting paper while they dry. The folds of the pages often need repairing, and this is done by pasting narrow strips of paper along them, an operation known as *back stripping*.

When the repair work is completed, the pages are re-folded with a bone or ivory *folder*, a simple item that may become curiously personal to the user. Then the sections are reassembled, taking great care that they are in correct order and checking by both page numbers and *signature marks*, which are the tiny capital letters or numbers put by the printer at the foot of each page commencing a section. The binder usually adds *fly leaves* at both ends of the book with the dual purpose of protecting the printed leaves and making a good attachment between text and covers; Mr Powell also incorporates a linen joint in these fly leaves for extra strength.

Sewing together the sections of the book is perhaps the most important operation in binding, since all subsequent stages and the behaviour of the

*Sections of a book being assembled on the sewing frame, using linen thread to sew them to the vertical cords. Later, the ends of the cords will be used to attach the front and back boards of the book.*

finished book depend upon it. But requirements vary. For example, it may be desirable for the spine of a book printed on stiff paper to *throw up* sharply when opened to allow the pages to be read, and this calls for a different kind of sewing from that for a book printed on thin paper. It is because he believes the structure of a book to be so important that Mr Powell has chosen the *sewing frame* as a house-symbol for his notepaper, showing a book sewn on cords, or thongs.

The frame has a wooden base supporting a screw-threaded pillar on each side, linked by an adjustable crosspiece. This serves to hold taut a number of vertical cords anchored below the front edge of the base. To these *cords* or *bands* (sometimes linen tapes or vellum strips) each section of the book is sewn at marked positions. The commonest number of cords is five, though a large volume may have seven and a small one only three. Their spacing is sometimes varied for decorative reasons, perhaps to echo the margins of the printed text or to relate to the cover design. Each section is sewn through its fold, both to the cords and to the previous section, so making a strong whole; linen thread is used in two parts, rubbed with beeswax to keep the strands together. The ridges formed by the sewing operation are the origin of the bands which are prominent on the spines of hand-sewn books. When the sewing is done, the cords are cut off leaving *slips* a few inches long.

Except for conservation binding (in which original edges are preserved) this is the stage at which the *fore-edge, head* and *tail* of the pages may be trimmed. For this purpose, the book is held in a *cutting press*, a large wooden clamp incorporating a plough cutter with horizontal blade; the book is held vertically in the press and very evenly trimmed as the blade is gradually screwed forward.

One thing about this coverless volume is soon apparent: because of the thread, it is thicker at the spine than at the fore-edge. This swelling is dispersed in an operation known as *rounding and backing*, by which the spine is manipulated to round it and the sections are then fanned out by tapping with a *backing hammer*. The result can be seen by examining the head and tail edges of many hard-backed publishers' bindings. It is usual to glue the section folds of paper-leaved books before rounding and backing, afterwards allowing the book to set between its *front board* and *back board*. The boards have a protective function and help to maintain the shape of the book; they are cut a little over the page dimensions, allowing a *square* to project at head, tail and fore-edge. Many early books were bound in wooden boards which are re-used when re-binding, and sometimes the binder must turn carpenter, making up the width where the original has shrunk. Boards are attached by lacing the ends of the cords through their inner edges.

In order to resist strain when a book is pulled off the shelf, *headbands* of strips of leather, vellum or cord are sewn at head and tail with thread or coloured silks; the stitches pass through the outermost holes of the sewn sections. The degenerate descendants of what is essentially a structural feature are sometimes seen today in those lengths of stuck-on headband applied to more expensive books: they are purely decorative.

Only now, after a strong, workmanlike construction has been made, is the book ready for covering. Leather is the traditional and most usual material and the binder selects and handles it with care, choosing a skin of thickness proportionate to the size of book. To avoid undue bulkiness at the edges and stiffness at the joints, the leather is pared down at those points, taking pains to avoid irregularities which might show up when the cover sets. The cover is stuck with boiled flour paste and the book is closed to draw the cover taut over the spine, bringing the cords into prominence; they can be further accentuated by pinching up with *band nippers. Headcaps* are formed where the back is turned in to cover the headbands. After covering, the volume is ready for *finishing*.

It is in the lettering and decoration of the cover that the binder has an opportunity to express his artistry, and he may employ many different materials, including coloured leather (inlaid and onlaid), metal, polished stones, embroidery and penwork. A series of volumes may be finished so that each forms part of a larger design when their spines or front boards are placed together. The matter of cover design is a large field, but it may be noted that in general the bookbinder aims to achieve a harmony between the claims of the book as a binding, as a piece of typography and as a literary work. Mr Powell pursues a simple approach to his designs with a clean, typographic emphasis; often he will use letters as a pattern, taken from the title or some phrase in the text.

Traditionally, *tooling* is the principal means of embellishment. *Blind tooling* produces simple impressions in the leather while *gold tooling* is done through gold leaf. In both cases the tools are used warm or hot. Broadly speaking, there are two kinds of finishing tool; those that are a complete small design, and those that are used as elements in making larger designs; for example, buds, blossoms and leaves which can make up flowers in various positions. The binder also needs sets of *gouges* (curved lines), *pallets* (straight lines), *fillets* (wheels producing a continuous line) and alphabets and numbers in various sizes. An attractive feature of gold tooling is the variable texture of reflection it presents. Mr Powell has built up an extensive collection of finishing tools over the years, many of them specially made. When a large block has to be used for some feature such as a coat of arms, it is applied to the book in a press; in common with a number of other binders, Mr Powell has adapted an antique 'Albion' printing press for this purpose, incorporating an electric element to heat the blocks.

The lettering and decoration to be executed are impressed on thin paper by inking the finishing tools on a stamp pad. This pattern is attached to the leather and the warm tools once again pressed through the paper to make their impressions on the leather. Most finishers use tools with individual handles but Mr Powell likes an interchangeable head system, heating the heads first on an electric boiling ring, then transferring them to the end of an adapted soldering iron, thermostatically controlled. During this work, the book is held steady in a small *finishing press*, or rested on a turntable on the bench top.

Work to be gold tooled is struck twice, the first time blind. This impression is painted with *glair* (white of egg or shellac) which is allowed to dry and then very lightly Vaselined. The gold leaf is tricky stuff to handle, being only about 1/250,000 inch thick. A piece is lifted from the maker's booklet onto a leather *gold cushion* and trimmed to size with a *gold knife*; it is picked up with a pad of cotton wool, slightly greased by passing it over the binder's head a couple of times, and placed in position, where

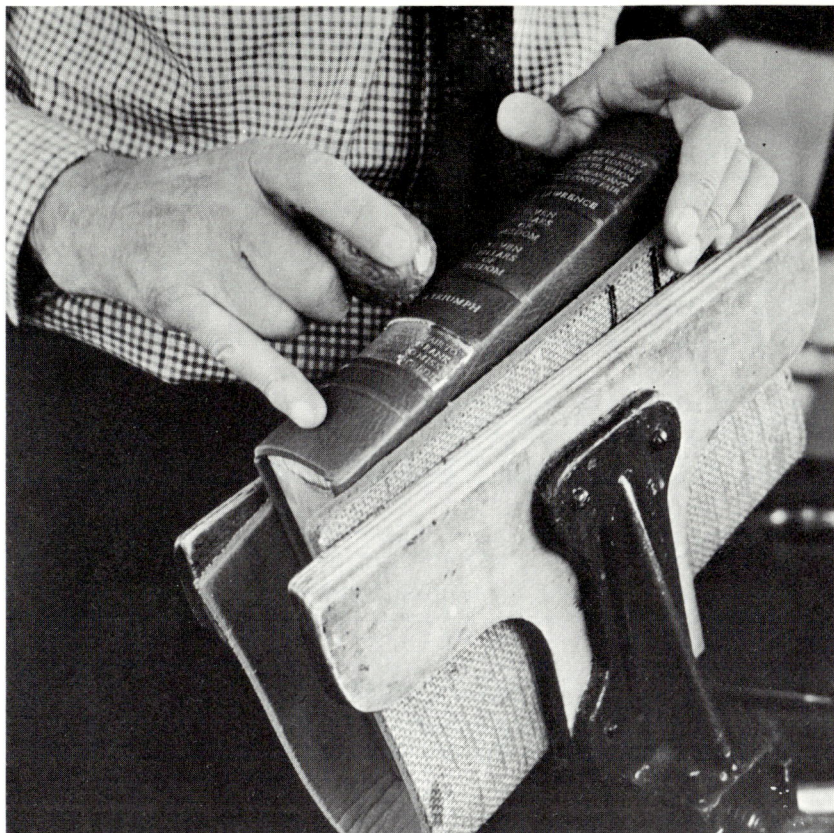

*Gold tooling and decoration is a relatively minor final stage in binding a book. The letters have been struck warm through the gold leaf and surplus is being removed with a gold rubber.*

it is held by the Vaseline. Then the work is struck a second time, and the glair softens to hold the gold leaf. Surplus gold is afterwards removed with a *gold rubber*, a ball of raw rubber soaked in paraffin. Lastly, the covers may be polished with a warm *polishing iron*.

Of all the fine and famous volumes Mr Powell has repaired and re-bound none, probably, is more renowned than the eighth-century Book of Kells kept in the Library of Trinity College, Dublin; it is one of the masterpieces of Celtic art. The book had last been bound in 1895 and was deteriorating badly, with pages detached, when Mr Powell was commissioned to re-bind it. As the book was considered too precious to leave the Library, the work on it meant spending three months in Dublin in 1953 and taking over a vanload of equipment.

What followed was a conservation saga that can only be outlined. After the book had been taken apart, it was carefully examined and the opportunity taken to build up a complete record of its condition. Many of the vellum leaves had cockled badly and needed to be flattened by damping, afterwards being left to dry under gentle tension from bulldog clips pegged out round the edges. A number of repairs were needed, one calling for the framing in new vellum of a decorated leaf which had at some time been cut back to the edge of the colour.

Folds which were weak or separated had to be strengthened and *guarded* with specially-woven linen strips, pasted and sewn. The sewing was neatly positioned by the marks of a transfer wheel and a total of about 16,000 stitches were put in. Back-stripping produced a considerable thickening of the section backs when re-folded, and this was balanced out by inserting additional plain vellum leaves on a small number of guards. However, the overall result was a bulk too unwieldy for one volume and a decision was taken to bind the four Gospels separately.

Sewing was done on five double cords incorporating headbands of unusual type and strength. Quarter-cut figured English oak was chosen for the boards and the slips glued and pegged into holes in them. The volumes were quarter-bound in alum-tawed pigskin, to which the headbands were also sewed for strength, and pigskin caps laid over at head and tail for additional protection of the spine against rubbing. A mahogany chest was made by Mr Powell's neighbour, the furniture maker Edward Barnsley, in which each volume lies flat in a drawer under light spring pressure to keep the leaves flat. Whenever the volumes are opened, wooden rollers are placed under the spines so that they will throw up without undue strain on the sewing.

It is a far cry from the Book of Kells to the well-thumbed dictionary or handbook of the average home, yet Mr Powell has not been above giving talks on how one may bind books on the kitchen table, using materials readily to hand. The two extremes present a common challenge, however: the need to think out what is required and how it should be done. His work is intended to be used, and in that lies the essence of craftsmanship.

# The furniture maker

Edward Barnsley of Froxfield has inherited a famous tradition of craftsmanship. His father Sidney, and his uncle Ernest, were both closely associated between 1890 and 1919 with one of the contemporary leaders in design, the architect Ernest Gimson who was himself directly inspired by William Morris. From 1894 to 1907 (during which period Mr Barnsley was born) the three friends worked at Pinbury Park near Cirencester and later at Sapperton, Gloucestershire. Here they were the principals in the Daneway Workshops whose austere style and superb craftsmanship made an outstanding contribution to the development of modern furniture design. Gimson was interested in the furnishing of houses and designed a great deal of furniture (which, like some of the notable furniture designers of earlier times, he did not actually make himself); Ernest Barnsley was an architect first and foremost; Sidney Barnsley was the master cabinet maker delighting to execute the pieces he designed.

Born into such an atmosphere of dedicated talent, it is hardly surprising that Mr Barnsley took up his father's work early. He can still remember making his first piece of furniture at the age of five – a stand for supporting a bucket at the pump. Later on he became a pupil at Bedales School, Steep, where there was a strong emphasis on studio and workshop practice, and he has always held that this had an important formative influence; it is surely more than coincidence that both Mr Barnsley and his near neighbour the bookbinder, Roger Powell, are old Bedalians. In Mr Barnsley's case the ties are especially strong, for some of the school buildings were designed by Gimson, and, after his death in 1919, Sidney Barnsley superintended the construction of the famous timber-framed library which was one of his last works. Yet another old Bedalian, Geoffrey Lupton, carried out the actual building work, and it was to him that Mr Barnsley was apprenticed when he left school. Three years later he went to study design at the Central School of Arts and Crafts, and then in 1923 when Lupton moved he launched into business on his own account in Lupton's workshop.

There he has remained ever since, though the workshop has been considerably enlarged and modified.

Mr Barnsley has thought a good deal about the factors which have helped to mould his career. The tradition inherited from his father is one, and so is the craft emphasis of his school; he believes that natural environment is another. He was born in a beautiful place, and after working for more than half a century in a beautiful corner of Hampshire he has come to the conclusion that it has not only been a privilege but a creative influence.

For a time, when he first began to make furniture, Mr Barnsley accepted the Gimson/Barnsley tradition unquestioningly, but then came to realise it was necessary to think things out for himself and develop his own style; a process stimulated by a period as design adviser at Loughborough College. Now, looking back, he can say, 'What I like to think I've done is in some measure to improve on two backgrounds or traditions. One is the Gimson/Barnsley with which I started, on to which I like to think I've built something new; the other is the eighteenth century, from which I now derive most of my plans and thoughts.' He adds, modestly, 'It's not for me to say if I've improved on the eighteenth century.' Traditional English design is certainly a strong feature of Mr Barnsley's work, with here and there hints of Daneway techniques in the use of inlays and contrasting panels. The rather suave Scandinavian approach which has affected so much furniture design of the post-war years has made little impact on him, and his work has a clean, often delicate, functionalism which is quite clearly his own.

The visitor looking for Mr Barnsley's workshop knows when he has arrived by the stacks of seasoning timber neatly arranged in open sheds beside the road, planks spaced to allow the free circulation of air. Some of it has been in stock for nearly fifty years, awaiting the right opportunity for which he knows it will one day be needed. Timber is all-important to him, and he is constantly on the look-out for really good stuff, straight-grained, free from knots, shakes and sapwood; in a word, 'clean'. Once, more than 80% of the timber he used was air-dried and English; now, almost 80% of it is kiln-dried and imported. That, of course, reflects the general situation in Britain today, 'where the supply of native timber has long ceased to meet demand, and explains why Mr Barnsley cherishes so carefully the remains of his stocks laid down in earlier years. The English woods he likes to use are walnut, chestnut, yew and cedar of Lebanon; oak less now than he did at one time. From overseas come Indian rosewood, Cuban mahogany and Australian black bean.

It is in understanding the properties of the various timbers, the ways in which they may be worked and the effects that may be achieved with

*Inlays of contrasting colour are a commonly-used form of furniture decoration. Their construction is made easier by the use of mechanical routers which cut out the hollow shapes; into these are glued slices of the profiled inlay wood.*

them, that much of the furniture maker's expertise lies. Sometimes the grain has curves which suggest a way in which it might be employed, sometimes the figuring can be used to decorative advantage. However, not all the timber used in Mr Barnsley's workshop is solid wood. Prepared boards such as chipboard, plywood and blockboard are used for backs and as a base for veneers, for some fine timbers are unobtainable in large widths and must be used sparingly when covering the surfaces of such pieces as chests, wardrobes and tables.

The essence of craft furniture making is fine quality hand joinery, so it may come as something of a surprise to find one room in the workshop containing a range of woodworking machines. It is interesting, moreover, to learn that they are not merely tolerated as a necessary evil but held to be a positive asset – in the right place. People tend to scorn the idea that a craftsman should use any kind of machine to further his ends, but Mr Barnsley does not subscribe to that attitude. 'There's always been a good deal of mythology about hand work,' is his rejoinder. 'We like to think

*An almost-finished chair in the workshop. Because chairs are commissioned in some quantity, it is economical to turn out a limited number of basic designs and modify them to suit individual requirements.*

that these machines we use are powered tools – we are not allowing them to deflect us from the main purpose.' Or put another way, the machine is being used as an extension of the craftsman's skill and work is not designed with the convenience of the machine in mind. So the circular saw, bandsaw, planing machine and spindle moulder are used to reduce profitless drudgery in preparing timber, leaving the craftsmen free to employ their skill where it will be truly significant. Of course, large pieces of wood can be sawn and planed by hand, but there is little point in expending time and energy on what can be done more easily and efficiently by machine.

These days, Mr Barnsley does little of the actual construction work himself; rather, like Ernest Gimson, he is the inspiration behind the furniture that bears his name. He designs his pieces sitting at a large drawing board in a rather bare office whose starkness is more than compensated for by one of the noblest views in Hampshire – the precipitous slopes of Stonor Hill seen across the garden and over the treetops. It is a setting which, if it does not directly inspire his work, certainly provides a calm and refreshing atmosphere for it. Mr Barnsley likes his designs to take shape rapidly because lack of spontaneity may produce a laboured effect. To satisfy himself that a piece will work well and be aesthetically pleasing, he makes perspective sketches and full-size detail drawings. Sometimes an apparently straightforward subject, such as a dressing table mirror stand, will pose finicky problems which can only be resolved with patient experiment.

With the design worked out, Mr Barnsley consults his foreman Bert Upton (whose life has been spent in the workshop), about suitable timber and production methods. Mr Upton selects and cuts the timber, using the machines to full advantage to prepare it to the bench stage; then it is passed on to the assistants. Each of the four men (there is sometimes a trainee as well) has his own tool chest which contains an extensive array of hand tools in liftout trays. Shop tools – elaborate or specialised ones – are provided for general use.

An article of furniture may contain a good number of different parts, all of which must initially be reduced to the right overall dimensions. A variety of saws is a first necessity – *cross-cut* and *panel saw* for larger pieces, *tenon saw* for smaller items. Fineness of cut depends on the number of points to the inch. Curved cuts, when required, may be made with the *bow saw* or the smaller *coping saw*, both having narrow blades and open frames to facilitate manoeuvrability. For basic truing of surfaces a *fore plane* is used on long pieces and a *smoothing plane* on shorter ones; the latter is also used for general cleaning-up work. A number of other planes may be useful in special circumstances, the *plough plane* (for cutting grooves), the *compass plane* (for working inside curves) and the *rebate plane*.

It is the next stage of work which is the real test of skill: making the joints. There are many different ones for different applications, and the furniture maker needs to know which are strongest and most appropriate for the piece in hand. On *case furniture* (chests, writing desks and the like) *dovetailing* is frequently employed both for its strength and its looks; on chairs and tables, varieties of the *mortise and tenon* are more usual for joining legs, stretchers and rails. The strength of a piece of furniture depends more on the accurate fitting of its joints than on any fastenings, so tools of finer cut are brought into use. The *dovetail saw* has more points to the inch, the *block plane* is used on smaller surfaces and across the grain, and the little *bullnose plane* can be worked in small spaces. Mortises and other joint housings are cut with chisels of appropriate width, while *try square*, *bevel* and *marking gauge* are used in setting out the joints.

Decoration is kept to the minimum on Mr Barnsley's furniture, purity of line and beauty of grain being its chief visual appeal. An inlaid line of

*Although machines may be used to take the drudgery out of preparing larger pieces of timber, it is skill at the bench with hand tools which produces really fine pieces of furniture. There is no better place for a trainee to discover the meaning of craftsmanship.*

contrasting colour often serves to define a shape; sometimes a simple roll moulding will be worked on an edge with a home-made *scratch tool*, which is a shaped steel blade in a wooden holder. After final assembly, pieces are generally finished with wax or teak oil. A heat-resistant lacquer is sprayed on some large pieces such as table tops.

Although all his furniture is made to order, Mr Barnsley likes to prepare a number of pieces to the same basic design and then modify them for individual customers; in this way there is a considerable saving on production costs, especially with chairs. Among commissions of recent years was one of the largest he has ever received – fifty-two chairs for an Oxford college. But his belief about the use of machinery still holds good: character comes from hand work, flatness of quality from the machine.

It is a tribute to Mr Barnsley's reputation that he needs no agents or retailers; customers find their own way to his quiet lane and collect their completed orders direct from the workshop door. Most of them are still discriminating private purchasers, although schools, colleges, churches, cathedrals and business houses are much in evidence; on the requirements of the last, for board rooms, prestige offices and dining rooms, the future seems likely to depend more heavily.

# The hand block printer

In sheltered workshops up and down the country, many handicapped people work at hand crafts with considerable success, despite obvious competition from the more fortunate: the blind basket makers are an example that comes readily to mind. A less common craft that deserves to be better known is the hand printing of textiles which is carried on at Yateley, a few miles from Sandhurst. Here some thirty-five women live and work together and make a range of products whose colourfulness is a brave defiance of the disabilities from which they suffer; among them there are spastics and amputees, sufferers from polio and spina bifida, and the greater number are mobile only in wheelchairs.

An Indian rajah's sick daughter was the unlikely cause of bringing the workshop into being, for it was when a young orthopaedic sister, Jessie Brown, went to India to nurse her that she first saw simple textile printing being carried on. It struck her that this could well be a profitable occupation for the disabled, so upon her return she sought out a friend whom she had nursed through polio and together they set up a tiny workshop in a garden shed. Here Jessie Brown and Grace Finch struggled to learn the techniques and sought inspiration from a small collection of textiles brought back from India. The experiment was promising enough to secure backing for the setting up of a small hostel and workshop for eight girls which opened in 1937, had to close on the outbreak of war and was re-opened in 1946. Through Miss Brown's continuing efforts, helped by a prominent surgeon and with government aid, the present substantial building was put up in 1952 and a group of specially-designed bungalows followed a few years later. Now, as Assistant Manager, the same Miss Finch leads a busy life overseeing the work of the cutting room, dye shop, block room, printing room, sewing room, boiler room and showroom, which today comprise Yateley Industries for Disabled Girls.

New textiles have their beginning in the block room, where the printing blocks are cut and prepared. Their designs may be created in a variety

*Fabric blocks are cut from lino panels, using carving tools to remove waste and leave the design standing in relief. The block is afterwards surfaced with flock so that it will hold the printing dye.*

of ways: sometimes by a professional designer, sometimes by one of the employees with artistic flair, sometimes by Miss Finch, who is always on the look-out for illustrations that will translate into another medium. But any good idea from the shop floor stands a chance of being adopted.

The design is drawn full size, with solid areas as they will finally appear, and a tracing is made by which the design can be transferred through carbon paper to the block. This is made of heavy quality lino, mounted on wood, and is cut with standard lino-cutting tools and craft knives; one of the women with special aptitude is kept busy on block cutting and there is now a collection of upwards of a thousand blocks which can be called on.

Printing directly on fabric with thin dyes produces a blotchy effect, so the face of the block must first be made absorbent by *flocking* it. Slow-drying white enamel paint is rolled evenly over it and finely-chopped wool flock powdered on through a sieve; after drying for two or three days the surplus is removed and the block is ready for printing. Blocks that have been much used require re-flocking to keep them in suitable condition.

Powdered chemical dyes are very carefully weighed and mixed in the dye shop according to a recipe book; any mistake made at this stage may not become apparent for several days, as the final colour is not seen until processing of the fabric is complete. The vehicle for the dye is gum tragacanth, prepared from powder form by first steeping in water for two days, then boiling for another two, until the evil-smelling substance has reached an easy flowing consistency. The addition of a *mordant* enables the dye to penetrate (literally, bite into) the fabric. A dye pad is needed – one for each colour to be printed – made from a square of wood covered with layers of felt, rexine and blanket. They are rinsed out after use and kept for subsequent jobs with the same dye.

Meanwhile, the materials to be printed are got ready in the cutting room. The outlines of standard items are drawn round cardboard templates and an electric cutter used to cut out many thicknesses at once. Unbleached cotton, linen, hessian, union cloth and muslin are among the most-favoured fabrics.

Fifteen or more women work in the printing room in three production teams, one of which is led by Anne Cox, whose circumstances are typical. She contracted polio in her teens, and although partial recovery left her able to work from a wheelchair, she found employment very difficult to get. It was with some misgivings that she came to Yateley for a trial but she has been happy to stay there for twenty years. Not all who come are accepted: there is a preliminary assessment to test aptitude for the work and compatability with the community, followed by a period of probation before training proper starts. Miss Cox realised, as others have, the importance of breaking the ties of protective sympathy and achieving independence, and although when she came she had no artistic inclinations, over the years she has developed an eye for colour and design.

The actual printing involves inking a block by pressing it on the pad (charged from the dye bottle with a brush), placing it on the fabric and tapping the back with a suitable weight; the workbench is covered, like the dye pad, to provide a resilient surface which will also absorb any surplus dye that soaks through the fabric. All but the smallest blocks get five taps, one for each corner and the centre. Old cast-iron dumb-bells – themselves rather decorative objects – have been found to serve admirably. It looks deceptively simple, and an experienced printer like Miss Cox works with a steady rhythm turning out as many as 5 yds of 36 in material a day. In practice, the job can be quite demanding for a handicapped person. Muscular control may be difficult at best and made more so by the complication of working at low level from a wheelchair; bench height is important as the repeated lifting and controlled placing of a 4 lb dumb-bell by a seated person can be quite tiring. Those who do it enjoy pointing

*By making two creases in the fabric the centre point of the article (a teacloth) is easily found. The block has to be carefully placed to ensure accurate register of the design.*

out that the total lifting power needed to print a 4 in square block all over a 5 yd length of 36 in material is actually equivalent to a small tonnage. Blocks up to about 12 in square can be printed by this method but are difficult to handle, so that most printers are happier with smaller sizes.

When a small item such as a teatowel or a headsquare is being printed with an all-over pattern it is usual to start at the centre – found by folding in half each way to make two creases – and work out to the edges, masking off any border with newspaper. The block has to be placed so that it registers exactly against the adjacent impressions. Where a design calls for the placing of blocks in open areas, even more careful judgement is called for and Miss Cox has become so adept that she never needs to measure the position. Many two-colour jobs are tackled, with some particularly pleasing effects being achieved by the double printing of open all-over designs.

Printing is followed by a short spell of drying on racks in a warm room, then the fabrics are parcelled up in old sheets to spend an hour and a quarter in a steam cupboard in the boiler room while the dye gets right into the fibres of the material. A hot wash removes the remaining gum

*A hand block printer at work, using a dumb-bell to produce a firm impression. Using smallish blocks, an output of about five square yards a day is achieved by disabled workers.*

tragacanth, and rinses in acetic acid and cold water then follow before drying and ironing.

A team of machinists in the sewing room make up the prints into a wide range of useful articles which includes aprons of several kinds, bedspreads, curtains, tablecloths, shirts, headsquares and triangles, ties, teatowels and much else. Rough textures like hessian often give most attractive results and garden aprons and cushion covers in this material sell well. Thin materials present something of a problem at Yateley as the usual practice is to stretch them out and work across the top, something that is not possible from a wheelchair; it has been found impractical, for the same reason, to attempt screen printing.

The workshops have their own showroom and also supply work to craft shops and galleries, some overseas. They are particularly well suited to short-run production of special commissions such as sets of garments or fabrics for interior designers. The technique of hand block printing makes for a pleasing 'folk' quality that is seen in both design and execution and has all the more appeal for its individuality.

# The potter

A dedication to usefulness might fairly be said to characterise Christopher Charman's life and work. Most of his pottery is intended for active service in the home, and that, he believes, is essentially what pottery is all about: for doing a job. Not for him exhibition galleries and small artistic circles, though his work is far from being dull. In adopting such a philosophy he has returned to the very roots of the craft, and works in the old tradition of the country potters, rather than that of the more common studio potters. He is a quietly-spoken yet down-to-earth man who enjoys a relaxed family life on the edge of the New Forest, and who somehow finds time to run a fifty-acre farm as well as a successful pottery venture.

Mr Charman's parents were keen craftworkers, and it was from his mother that he learned the rudiments of pottery. Later, while at school in Devon, he used to pay frequent visits to the old-established Clevedon pottery, and it was there that he was stimulated to take it up as a hobby. When eventually he came back to the family home it was primarily to buckle down to the challenging task of reclaiming a patch of rough land and making it support him. Potting at this stage was a rather uncertain affair, but Mr Charman approached it with similar determination. He was hampered by lack of facilities, the most serious deficiency being any means of firing a kiln. The nearest electricity supply was some way away, and that meant siting his kiln near the mains in a friend's garden and making frequent trips in the night to attend to it. Glazing his pots called for hazardous trips down the road with a bucket of glaze balanced on the handlebar of his motor cycle. However, it was all useful experience and taught him much; and at the same time he was reading books on potting, deriving particular benefit from the writings of that doyen of British potters, Bernard Leach.

The 1950s, when Mr Charman eventually decided to begin selling his wares, were a good time to be setting up as a potter, for the austerity of the post-war years was passing, more spending money was becoming available, and public interest in hand work was growing. The great number of studio potters who have set up in business in the last two decades confirms how this trend has continued, and interest in potting is fostered by many schools and part-time classes. For a few years, Mr Charman went into partnership with a fellow potter and together they built a workshop and two wooden showrooms. His reputation is now well established and customers in plenty pull off the road to park on the grass outside the wooden house at Godshill. There is no need to advertise, to exhibit in shows or sell to shops, which is the kind of advantage that comes from being situated in a popular amenity area.

Another advantage of Mr Charman's location is the natural occurrence of suitable potting clay on his own land. In these days, when transport is easy and potters everywhere can get their clay ready-prepared from commercial suppliers, this is not of any great importance; but in the past it was one of the crucial factors in the siting of a pottery, the other being a supply of suitable fuel. In fact, Mr Charman gets most of his ball clay (so-called from the form in which it was supplied in the eighteenth century) from Devon, four tons at a time, dried and powdered, but mixes one-third of his own with it. About once every three years he digs out a supply quite near the workshop and allows it to weather until wanted for use. Handling large quantities of clay is an unavoidable chore; each week he must keep the supply up, by preparing the two or three hundredweight which is his regular consumption and which has to be kept for a month to develop full plasticity. A welcome aid in the laborious process is a baker's dough mixer, popular with many potters, into which goes a hundredweight of local clay to be stirred with water for at least two hours until a fine slurry is formed. Then it goes into a tub to settle and surplus water is siphoned off. Having reached the consistency of thick mud, the clay goes back into the mixer and the white ball clay is added, to be stirred in for about twenty minutes; after this, the clay can be knocked into lumps for storing in dustbins.

It should, of course, be made clear that the composition of a pottery body can be varied a good deal according to the type of ware being made and the result sought; in addition to clays it may include ingredients to help it withstand high firing temperatures, such as flint, quartz, sand and *grog* (ground-up fired clay), and ingredients to promote fusion, like felspar and Cornish stone. At the same time, their inclusion can have an interesting influence on the texture of the finished pot.

One further stage of preparation is needed before the clay begins its actual transformation into a pot: *wedging*, which is carried out immediately before use. Taking a lump of about ten pounds weight, Mr Charman works it round and round, pressing heavily on it with the ball of both

*Potting is more energetic than might appear at first sight. Every week in this workshop some hundredweights of clay have to be prepared, and immediately before use the clay must be wedged for a hundred turns to expel air bubbles.*

hands so that it forms a kind of shallow cone. By the time he has given it a hundred turns it will be of even working consistency and any air bubbles well and truly squeezed out. Methods of doing the job vary; this particular technique originated in Japan and is now used by many western potters. If Mr Charman is going to make a series of similar pots (and he makes many articles in dozen multiples) he will weigh the clay out in balls, to be sure that the finished pieces all have the same bulk.

Now it is time for the creative work. There are three foot-cranked *kick wheels* against the workshop windows, each one incorporating a seat and a shallow triangular tray to catch waste clay and water spillage; pottery throwing is far from clean as the bespattered windows testify. Seating himself on the bench, Mr Charman turns the wheel quickly and places a ball of clay firmly in the centre, using both hands, well wetted, to position it properly. It is important to do this *centring* well, as, if the clay is drawn up while off-centre, a lop-sided pot and a collapse will be the outcome. The spinning mound is opened up by inserting the right index finger in the centre while the clay is steadied by the left hand; and the hole is enlarged with gentle pressure. Changing hands, the pot is drawn up, controlled by the finger tips or knuckles as necessary. As anyone who has been to pottery classes knows, this apparently simple operation needs a lot of practice since disaster can easily result. All the time, the hands must be kept wet to lubricate the process.

If an upright pot is being made, the walls are drawn up to a cylinder and have to be compressed at the top, defying centrifugal force if a narrow-necked shape is called for. This is a tricky operation, in which the pot can easily go off-centre or develop an uneven rim. Of course, every potter has knacks which help with shaping; like using an old knife for example, when making a vessel with an over-hanging body which leaves no room for the fingers. When making a series of identical pots, the rim height and diameter can be checked with an adjustable marker fixed to the bench behind the wheel. The finished pot is removed from the wheel by slicing under its base with a cheese-cutting wire and is then very carefully placed on a rack to start drying off. If a handle is wanted, it is made by *milking* out from a pear-shaped ball of clay with a wet hand a long 'rope', which is nipped off as required. The top end is smeared upside-down onto the wall of the pot, looped over a finger and smeared on again at the lower end: it calls for a deft touch.

The basic pot has been shaped, but it is far from finished. Most of Mr Charman's output is slip-coated earthenware, and his next job is to apply the slip – finely-sieved clay and water into which the pot is completely or partly dipped, according to the effect sought. Then the pot can either be allowed to dry before receiving brush decoration with a metallic oxide, or it can be decorated with slip of a contrasting colour while still wet. A favourite method of Mr Charman's is to pipe on the design with a cattle hypodermic attached to a plastic bottle, rather like piping a cake decoration. The pot must be re-centred on the wheel if regular lines round the circumference are wanted. Regardless of decoration, every pot must be allowed to dry out slowly and naturally before it goes into the kiln for firing, for the same reason as bricks must be – to remove excess moisture which would cause the pot to explode in the intense heat of the kiln. In the warm climate of the workshop, the pots wait until they become *leather hard*, and at this stage it is possible to turn them to make a foot-ring, perhaps, or a cork hole in a cruet pot. The pot is re-centred, upside-down and secured with blobs of clay, and as it spins an iron cutting tool is brought up to it; the clay curls off in shavings very much as wood does.

Pots visit the kiln twice, the first time for the *biscuit* firing. Mr Charman has an electric kiln of 5 cu.ft capacity and another of 35 cu.ft capacity which he built himself. The kiln is packed as economically as possible to ensure that no space is wasted, and the odd corners are filled with small

*Drawing up a pot. The hands are kept wet while gentle pressure is applied to raise the walls. If the clay has not been accurately centred, disaster can easily result at this stage.*

items, such as pendants, which are ready sellers. The heat is slowly raised until, looking through the peephole, the pots are seen to be glowing red; then the temperature is turned up to about 950°C. This firing process lasts a total of some twenty-four hours, after which the kiln is allowed to cool for a similar period before opening.

The second or *glost* firing is to fire the glaze and seal the porosity of the earthenware. The glaze may have various constituents according to the potter's preferences and the effect he is seeking, with the addition of copper oxide producing a green finish, iron oxide brown, and tin oxide white. A favourite product of Mr Charman's is majolica ware, which exploits the rich colouring possible with glazes. The pot is first dipped in white glaze which quickly dries into the biscuit surface, and is then overpainted with brushwork or piping, in coloured glazes. It is a slow process, as the first glaze absorbs moisture from the brush while the decoration is being applied, and a set of twelve goblets can take a whole morning to do. When the glaze and final decoration have been applied the pots are fired for the second time, to 1140°C for twelve hours. Pyrometric cones placed in the kiln melt and indicate when the required temperature has been reached.

Earthenware and stoneware are the two most popular wares made in smaller workshops, and most of the foregoing account, while no more than an outline, covers a process common to them both. Stoneware, however, differs in being fired to a much higher temperature (1300°C) and thus needs a body containing more of those ingredients which help it to withstand greater heat and help fusion. It is a much harder product than earthenware, non-porous without glazing, and much used for ovenware. In the making, it has a way of being a good deal less predictable than earthenware, as Mr Charman points out: 'Stoneware, particularly, is exciting, because the fire gets between you and the pot and produces some unintended effects, often enhancing the pot.'

Not until the very last moment does he know how his work has fared. 'Opening a kiln after the glaze firing never loses its savour . . . it's always exciting.' He calls it, aptly, the potter's moment of truth. It is not difficult to understand the fascination which potting has come to have over the years for Mr Charman, or his respect for a material which can be handled in so many ways and be transformed from mud into something beautiful and hard as stone. No wonder that his farm tends to get in the way.

# SURVIVING CRAFTS

# The brick moulder

Few simple objects of everyday use could seem less likely to be the result of hand production than the humble brick. Millions are turned out daily, the annual consumption is enormous, the demand unceasing; and yet, here and there brickyards still actually prosper, doing by hand something that machines do more efficiently and cheaply. The reason is that the hand-moulded facing brick, variable in consistency and fired in small quantities, has characteristics of form, texture and colour which are not achieved in mass-production. While overall dimensions remain fairly constant, the surface has a rough sandy finish often showing the folding of the clay, and the colour may be red, yellow, brown, blue or purple depending on conditions in the kiln. The handling and burning of the bricks often result in slight warping and irregularities.

Perhaps it is not surprising then, that the hand-made brick has considerable appeal for discriminating architects. A brickyard at Michelmersh is now the last one in Hampshire to include such bricks among its output, and the men who work there are proud to claim among the buildings faced with their bricks the Nuffield Theatre at Southampton University, Salisbury shopping precinct, Romsey Magistrates' Court and Winchester Health Centre. A considerable amount of business is also done in connection with the restoration of old buildings, for they will make any shape or style of brick to order and in small quantities – something one could not expect from a large firm. The bricks are known as *Hampshire stocks*.

Bill Mason is one of three brothers who work at the Michelmersh yard and he has many years' experience behind him as a brick moulder. Born before the First World War, he began helping his father, also a moulder, at the age of ten during the school holidays; he was given the job of *plaiting-in*, rolling the clay ready for moulding. When he left school four years later, brick making was his first choice of job, but it was not until after the Second World War that he finally settled to it, after spells in building, engineering, forestry and the regular army. He saw active service in the War and was one of the lucky ones taken off the beaches at Dunkirk. Now he is content to stay at a job which during his lifetime has changed from being a hard way of earning a living to one with some positive advantages: 'It's quite a steady old number,' he says. 'Nobody to worry you; as jobs go these days it's not a bad job.'

When Mr Mason first took up the work much brick making was done out of doors and the *pug* (a mixture of clay and coal dust) was turned by one man with a *turning iron* while another trod it with bare feet. The moulders worked at their benches under improvised shelters, and it is hardly to be wondered at that in bad weather they preferred to exchange the inclemency of the yard for the comfort of the nearest hostelry. According to Mr Mason, 'They used to say that half the bricks were made in the pub.'

Conditions today are very much better and the Michelmersh yard has long been an 'inside' one, but brick production in the preparatory stages still has a primitive look about it. Clay is excavated by a crawler dragline in spring and autumn from a digging area about eight acres in extent; the operation produces a glutinous landscape in which movement on foot is impossible without rubber boots for seven months of the year, and then only just. The clay is left in heaps to weather for up to six months until it has lost its stickiness and is fit for use.

The dragline operator is also responsible for mixing the weathered clay with breeze (coal dust) from a tip near the moulding shed; it is needed to make the bricks burn in the kiln and the proportion included (which should be about 10%) largely determines the darkness of the finished product. In practice it is far from consistent, but this is in the nature of handmade bricks. With the dragline scoop, sticky masses of the mixture are dropped into the hopper of the pug mill next to the shed, and are there thoroughly mixed and any stones squeezed out; if stones were left in, the bricks would split when being fired. The mixed clay and breeze, now called pug, is brought by a short conveyor and screw elevator up to a level somewhat above the moulding benches. It is forced out of the elevator mouth looking like square, grey toothpaste, and is cut off with a wire and carried in armfuls to each moulder as required, being dropped on the bench to his right. A lad is kept busy supplying the five moulders who work one behind the other.

To watch Mr Mason at work is to be fascinated by the machine-like rhythm of his movements. From the heap of pug on his right he scoops up a large double handful and slaps it down on the bench over the surplus from the previous brick. He *plaits* it into a *walk*, rolling it in two directions, and throws it firmly into the mould, end-on to him in the middle of the bench. The clay spreads to fill the mould and the surplus is cut through

*The moulder throws the walk of clay into the mould just hard enough to fill the corners but not to obscure the folds which are a distinctive feature of handmade bricks.*

with a bentwood wire bow kept ready for use behind the mould. With a quick dab of his left hand in a heap of fine sand on the same side, Mr Mason scatters a little over the top of the surplus which he removes and throws on the bench (the sand prevents the clay from sticking to it). Now he lifts the mould, tips the contents deftly onto a small *pallet board* and places it on a plank to the left of the bench. This is still known as a *table barrow*, a reminder of the days when a hand barrow with table-like top was used to carry off the bricks for drying. The mould is well dusted in the sand heap and replaced on the bench where it fits over a bottom piece shaped so as to impart the *frog*, or indentation for cement.

From this description it will be seen that nine movements are involved in the making of every brick, carried out with great speed and deftness. A similar sequence has probably been followed since the earliest days of the craft and has been so refined that no further economy of movement is possible. One or two moulders work with such total absorption in the rhythm that their whole bodies spring from the feet like sparring boxers as the process is followed through.

From time to time Mr Mason makes use of three other items resting on a pile of bricks behind the mould: an old table knife kept for cleaning out the mould when it starts to become clogged, a small hoe-like *table scraper* to clean the bench, and a saucepan of water for sprinkling the bench so it can retain a dusting of sand. Steel moulds are used for standard bricks and wooden ones are readily made when special sizes or shapes, such as *splayed headers*, *squints* or *bull-nose copings*, are called for. Extra small bricks are made for fireplace work, some aptly known as *ladies' heels*. With all of them an allowance has to be made for shrinkage in drying.

After Mr Mason has turned some sixteen or seventeen bricks onto their pallet boards he uses another wet board to pick them up, sandwich-wise, and transfer them to the pallets of an adjacent rack. When five pallets have been filled, a *finger cart* running on rails past the ends of the moulders' benches lifts them in a group and carries them to the nearby drying tunnels. Ledges in the sides of these long brick chambers allow the pallets to be stacked mechanically, and when some 7000 of the *green* bricks are inside, wooden shutters are put up and hot air from the last kiln to be fired is circulated round them for three to five days. Unless most of their moisture is removed in this way, the bricks are liable to break up during burning.

When dry, the bricks are moved with another finger cart by the *outside gang* to one of the four kilns. These look like a cluster of domed, red-brick Mongolian tents, each about 30 ft in diameter and 12 ft high inside. Each holds about 35,000 bricks and packing them inside is tedious work, taking several days. Two men work together building up the bricks in stacks known as *baulks*, spaced slightly to allow the most effective circulation of heat.

*Each brick, as it is made, is deftly tipped onto a pallet board for ease of handling. Behind the moulder is his bench with its pile of fine dusting sand.*

*When the bricks have spent a period in the drying tunnel to remove moisture, they go to the kiln to be burned. They are stacked systematically in baulks, leaving passages for the circulation of heat.*

When all are snugly packed in – with little room wasted – the entrance is sealed up with a double wall of wasters filled with sand and rendered with clay. The roof, too, is coated with clay slurry and the vent bricked over.

Formerly the kilns were coal fired, but now it is crude oil, 700-800 gallons of it, that sets the bricks burning and raises the temperature inside the kiln to 1200°C. A glance through the peephole, a length of pipe left in the sealing, is awesome. After about thirty-six hours the oil is turned off, the breeze in the bricks is well and truly alight, and a blue haze pervades the atmosphere outside. Five days later the entrance is opened and a wait begins for enough heat to dissipate before the bricks can be *drawn* – another two to seven days. Shifting them is a hot job, hard on the hands, and they usually go straight onto the builder's lorry, unless they have to be graded for colour.

How many bricks does a moulder turn out in a day? The number varies with the individual and is reckoned to be between 1000 and 1400. 1000 bricks *an hour* has more than once been recorded elsewhere in the past, presumably as a feat of skill, while an old description of the craft states

*A wide variety of shapes is obtainable with hand-moulded bricks. In this picture the small bricks and the two central ones are for fireplace work; on the left is a double cant (for copings), on the right a plinth stretcher.*

that 'A handy man could mould in one day, viz., from five in the morning until eight at night, 5000.' He was indeed a handy man who worked a fifteen-hour day, but it must be added that such results were only achieved with the help of a team of assistants, which might include one to feed the pug, another to do the plaiting-in, a boy to empty the moulds and two to wheel away the bricks.

Today, the men who work at this increasingly uncommon craft form something of an elite, knowing how much their products are sought after. They are paid on a piecework rate which reflects their greatly improved status: when Mr Mason started as a lad the rate was 15/- (75p) a thousand – now it is well over £5. The moulders enjoy a good deal of freedom with regard to the hours they work and in this must lie much of the appeal of the job. Mr Mason believes it can also lead to a rather casual attitude, and if a man comes in late for work and then knocks off early in the afternoon, a terse explanation has been devised: 'We say the Isle of Wight man comes over,' (that is, he's got so far to travel he can't be expected to do much while he's here).

# The broom squire

'The men who make besoms', wrote an observer more than half a century ago, 'are always kindly and genial, and enjoy talking about their work.' (FitzRandolph, H. E. and Hay, M. D. *The Rural Industries of England and Wales*, 1926. Vol. 1 p.152.) The remark might seem to be nothing more than an easy generalisation, so it is pleasant to find it still holding good for one of the makers today. Peter Burrows is just that sort of man, always ready to chat about his work and explain its finer points, and it is not unusual for strollers and mothers with their children to stop and watch him through his workshop door and pass the time of day.

Following in the footsteps of his father and several earlier generations, he has been making brooms all his life; in fact, since he began helping at the age of five. That was in the 1920s, when brooms sold for a mere 8d (4p) each. Perhaps the returns from broom making have never been very high, which may be why Mr Burrows' father also worked on the railway and he himself has a part-time job as a groundsman. Nevertheless, he has a deep attachment to the work, enough to hope that one of his sons will take it up in due course and keep the family tradition alive.

How did the broom squire get his name? Mr Burrows suggests it could have been an indication of his unique job in the rural community, though this can hardly have applied in some of those villages on the Hampshire/Berkshire border where there used to be several; probably it was just a bit of pompous jocularity. He knows of another, less common title: the *broom dasher*. At one time, he recalls, makers would travel about (bowler hatted!) by pony trap, selling their wares from door to door, and it seems they must have acquired a reputation for being speedy salesmen.

The heathlands typical of northeast Hampshire and adjoining regions of Berkshire, Surrey and Sussex have long supported broom making, for this is the natural habitat of the raw materials – heather and the birch tree. The Hindhead area was once well known for its broom squires but now Mr Burrows can think of only a couple within a radius of many miles.

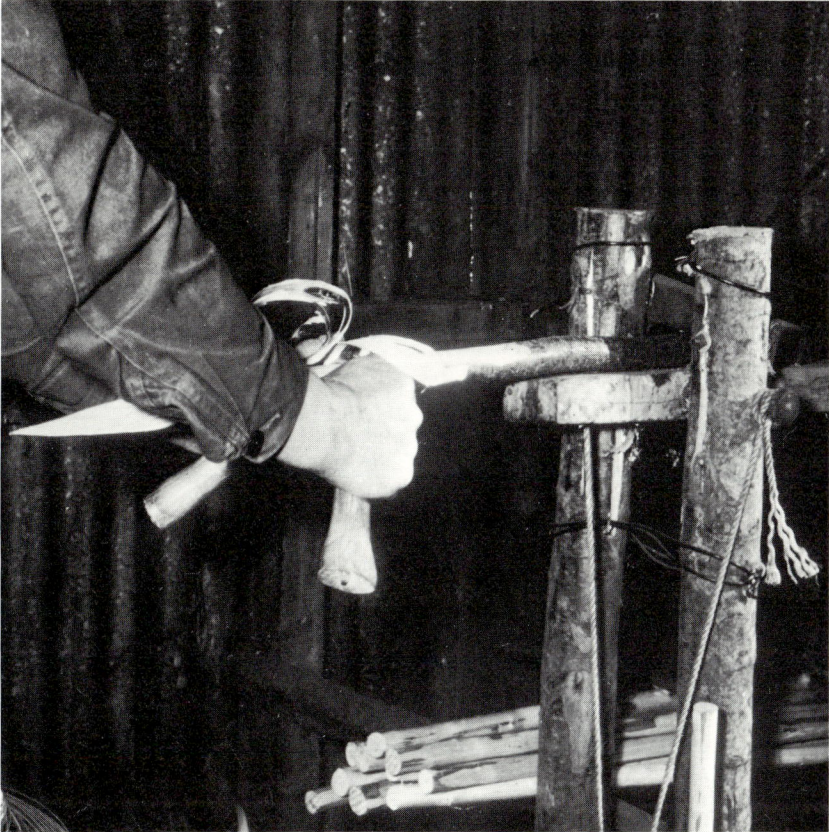

*A strong but simple brake holds a pole firmly while bark and knots are stripped to make a broom handle. The tool used is a curved draw-knife known as a broom handle shave.*

Gipsies, too, used to carry on the work – it has the merit of small overheads – but it is doubtful if any production continues among travellers.

While he still makes some heather brooms, traditionally used in hop kilns, Mr Burrows works mostly with birch, preferring the red to the silver variety which has a floppy, and therefore rather unsatisfactory, habit of twig. It needs to be about seven or eight years old, and can be cut as soon as the leaf comes off, usually after about the middle of October. His supplies in recent years have come from a place so whimsically named that it might have been invented as the setting for some rural farce: the Land of Nod, near Headley. He gets about 450 bundles of birch from an acre, enough to keep him going for a working year.

After felling the birches with a power saw and axe, armfuls of the twiggy material are bundled up in the fork of a sawing horse and tied with a thin hazel withy. To do this, one end is twisted back on itself to form a loop and the other is passed through and pulled tight round the bundle; two or three twists secure it. The cordwood remaining is sold off so there is little waste. As well as birch for the heads, Mr Burrows needs hazel, birch, ash or chestnut for the handles, preferring the last because it peels best.

A large, corrugated-iron shed not far from his home at Grayshott serves Mr Burrows as a workshop, and here he brings his raw materials with a Land Rover and trailer. Three or four months' seasoning is required before use, and while wood for handles can be stacked outside, the birch must be kept dry lest exposure make it too brittle. At one time it was not uncommon to see high stacks of birch in a country broom squire's yard, roofed with sloping bundles to keep off rain and sun; but if there is a capacious shed it is simpler to pack it all inside.

In making a broom handle, the pole is sawn to a length of 4 ft, using a notched piece of wood as a guide; any knots are trimmed with a small axe and one end is given a four-sided point, which will minimise twisting in the head. So that it is smooth to the hands in use, the bark is taken off with a *broom handle shave* which is like a small draw-knife whose blade is curved to fit round the pole. While the pole is being shaved it is held steady in a home-made *brake* built against the side of the shed; its angle-iron jaws are worked by foot-operated cords.

Twigs for the head are cut to about 3 ft long and sorted into two piles, coarse and fine, on either side of the *broom horse*. This useful device is simply a stool about 5 ft long with a foot-operated clamp at one end, and variations of it are used in several crafts where it is necessary to hold the workpiece steady and leave both hands free. Mr Burrows has neatly adapted his horse to suit his method of working. A little way from the head end he has fixed a crosspiece about 2 ft long, on the upper side of which are four curved forks to support the broom head. Sitting astride the horse, he places two leather straps over the crosspiece and puts a handful of coarse twigs in the forks; this is followed by a handful of fine twigs, then more coarse. The *nose* of fine material is thus encased in the coarse, and the whole lot is done up tightly in the two straps ready for binding. This used to be done with bark strip, split bramble or cane, but like most other makers Mr Burrows now finds galvanised wire more convenient. A reel of wire is held in a stand in front of the horse and fed under the wooden clamp. The end is tucked into the broom head about 6 in from the butt end and wound round it three times by turning the head and straining tight against the clamp. The wire is cut, the end bent, turned under twice, pulled tight and tucked in. Another binding is made 3 in

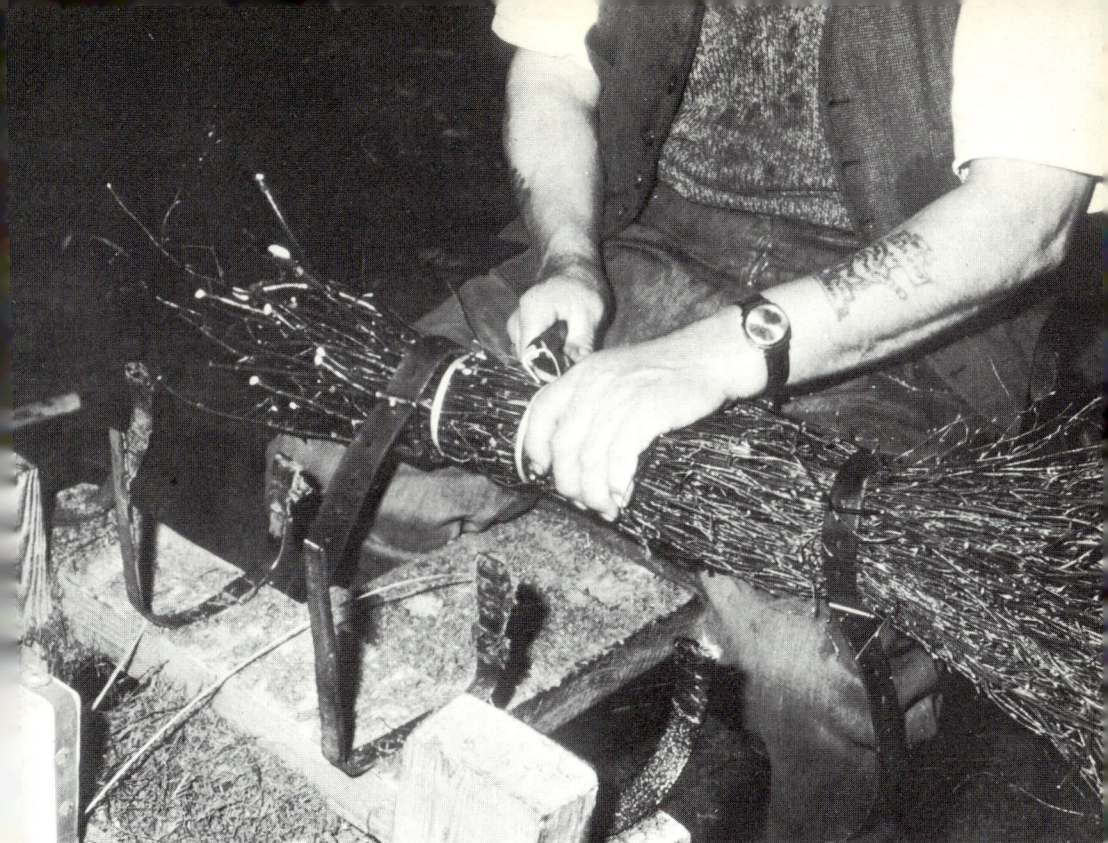

*The broom head is made from a bundle of selected birch twigs, held temporarily by two straps until the wire bindings are fastened. In some parts of the country the traditional thin wood strip bonds are still used.*

along and then the straps are removed and the butt trimmed off on the chopping block with the axe.

Heads are made one day, handles the next, and when a good stock is ready, assembly begins. A handle is nicked with a knife about 9 in from the point, to indicate depth of insertion, and the point started in the head; then, holding the broom upside-down, the handle is banged smartly on the block to ram it home. In this way the twigs in the head are packed even more tightly together. Most makers are then content to knock in a nail to stop the handle pulling out, but Mr Burrows believes in making a really secure job by driving a split wooden peg right through. He bores a hole with his *broom bit* (only the second specialised tool he uses), a short auger with a home-made handle, which is then used as a mallet to tap home the peg. The ends are trimmed off with a knife and all looks neat and workmanlike.

A broom ought to give at least a year's service with fair use, remembering that it is best used with a sideways, rather than an upright, sweep. Those that Peter Burrows makes sell over a wide area of Hampshire, Surrey and

*To make sure the handle will not pull out of the head, this maker secures it with a wooden peg. The handle of his broom bit serves as a mallet to tap the peg home.*

Sussex, though you have to give rather more for them today than when he first started. His work is more distinctive than might be supposed, and it was with some pleasure that the author was able to identify an anonymous broom seen in a south-coast hardware store as coming from his very hands.

Despite his familiarity with the work, Mr Burrows is at a loss when it comes to accounting for one old piece of broom-lore: Why is it that witches are supposed to use broomsticks as a means of transport? His ready rejoinder is that of the practical craftsman: 'I've made a good many, but never took off!'

# The cooper

One of the trades that is dying before our very eyes is that of the cooper or barrel maker, and it is a sad demise because this ancient craft has been of incalculable value. There is archaeological evidence that vessels of stave construction were being made in this country *c.* 200 BC and among the finds of casks from Roman Britain were some from the 1897 excavations at Silchester which had been used with their heads knocked out as well linings. Remains of casks were found with the treasures of the Anglo-Saxon cenotaph ship at Sutton Hoo. Incidentally, the term cask is to be preferred, as strictly speaking a barrel is a cask of 36 gallons capacity.

The cooper was useful for centuries to all kinds of trades and did not seriously begin to be displaced until the end of the last century. In the brewing industry he was secure until the end of the Second World War, when several factors began to tell against his craft. Chief among them was the need to find a container that could be more easily sterilised, since an ever-weakening brew encouraged the growth of certain bacteria in wooden casks; the cost and shortage of good timber ran it a close second. Metal casks began to be developed and then systems of bulk delivery, which in many cases made even these unnecessary. Not only coopers, but also connoisseurs of beer have regretted the change, and those who regard themselves as qualified to pass judgement reckon that beer out of metal containers just doesn't have the same flavour.

Although machinery for making beer casks was being developed in the 1880s and was installed on a large scale in some places, the coopers never found it much of a threat to trade. For one thing, it was expensive, and for another, casks were required in a great many sizes; it turned out that machine-made casks were no cheaper than those made by hand. And since wooden casks need a good deal of maintenance which machines cannot tackle, the coopers were still in demand. Theirs must be one of the very few hand trades which survived the advent of machinery and continued to flourish despite it.

We usually think of coopering as a highly-specialised part of the brewing trade, but that is only because its other forms have died out, though they were still active within living memory. This chapter is about the work of the *wet cooper*, making watertight casks, mainly used for beer, wines and whisky, though some are also made for substances such as sauce and vinegar. More than seventy different sizes were made for the wine trade at different times.

The second main branch of the trade was that of the *dry cooper*, who made a cheaper and less substantial cask. For a long time, casks were the most convenient way of transporting many dry goods and great numbers of coopers were to be found at work in seaports. They would sail in merchant ships with quantities of unfinished staves to make up for the cargo to be taken on, and they acquired the reputation of being a hard-drinking and hard-swearing lot. Dry casks were generally held together with hoops of split hazel and the need for these hoops gave rise to yet another craft that has now vanished. Casks used for commodities such as butter, soap and herrings needed to be rather better, and were known as *dry-tight casks*. The introduction of alternative forms of packaging was responsible for putting most of the dry coopers out of business but tobacco coopers were still busy after the Second World War.

The third branch of the trade was the *white coopers*, making buckets and tubs for domestic and industrial use, and butter churns and flower pots. Their work was in demand where metal containers would have been unsuitable for various reasons.

It is doubtful if there is more than a handful of coopers all told working in Hampshire today. One of them is Jan Swigoniak, whose skill is deeply rooted in his family background: many generations of his forebears were coopers before him. He was born in Berlin of Polish parents just after the First World War and admits to being fascinated by the work from an early age. He was apprenticed for three years to a master cooper on leaving school and eventually came to Britain in 1948. For the reasons which have already been outlined it was not the best of times for the cooper's trade, and in the circumstances it must have required some courage to set up in a strange country. Now he runs a small independent business with one assistant, adapting his skills to the possibilities of the times. There is very little demand for the making of new casks (except the small ones sought by enthusiastic home brewers) but there is still a steady call from the breweries for repairs; he undertakes work for one of the old-established county breweries and for cider makers in the West Country. The yard of his workshop at Netley Marsh is stacked high with casks awaiting attention and with piles of staves, heads and hoops, for there is no point in wasting seasoned components which can be re-used or adapted for other purposes.

But although Mr Swigoniak, like workers in several of the older trades, is not often called on to exercise the full scope of his craft, it is still necessary for him to have it at his fingertips, both to know what maintenance a cask requires and to carry it out. The following account of making a cask (simplified here and there) may serve to show just what skill is involved.

Oak is the only timber that satisfies the cooper's requirements as to working, hard wear, imperviousness and neutral taste, and the very best used to come from the Baltic regions of Russia and Poland: it was known as Memel oak, after the principal port of shipment. After the Second World War, it became prohibitively expensive and alternative supplies were got from Yugoslavia, North America and Iran. Trees are felled in winter and the trunks cut into approximately stave lengths. These are then quartered and cleft radially from the heart into rough staves; obtained in this way there is no subsequent warping. Traditionally, the staves are seasoned for anything up to five years, but today most are kiln-dried.

Making a cask falls into eight main stages of which the first is by far the most important, since upon the *dressing* or shaping of the staves will depend the size and efficiency of the finished article. After cutting to the correct length, the staves are first *listed*, that is, roughly tapered and the edges angled; if they are cleft, this is done with a broad axe on the *block*, a substantial section of tree trunk standing on end. Sawn staves are listed with a *draw-knife* while clamped in a *horse* on which the cooper sits. Next, the backs are curved off with the same tool and the reverse sides of the staves are given a concavity with a *hollow knife* similar to the draw-knife. Long staves are more easily dealt with by wedging them against a hook set in the side of the block. To finish the staves, their edges are planed on the *jointer*, a giant plane about 6 ft long; as it is too big to be used in the normal way it is used upside-down, supported at one end, and the staves are pushed over the iron. The angle at which the stave edges are planed is the radius of the finished cask, and accuracy is therefore most important. Staves which fail to meet correctly on inner or outer edges are described as *inshot* or *outshot* respectively, and only long experience can ensure that they will be just right. The jointing process also imparts a curve to the edges that determines the amount of *belly* the cask will have.

When the staves have been prepared they are *raised up*, or stood in a circle on end within a *raising-up hoop* which is hammered tight on to their upper ends. A stout *truss hoop* of ash is now hammered well down the staves, holding them secure; an iron *bulge hoop* goes on below the raising-up hoop and the truss hoop can be removed. The cask at this stage looks somewhat like an opening bud held by the two hoops at one end.

The next stage is *trussing up* the cask: bending the staves to their final position. In bigger workshops the raised-up cask may be softened by

*After one end of the part-made cask has been hooped, it is stood over the burning cresset for the heat to soften the staves. Successively smaller truss hoops are then hammered down to bring the open staves together, allowing the other chime hoop to be fitted. The process is here being repeated for the quarter hoop.*

steaming or immersion in boiling water, but a similar effect can be achieved by wetting the staves and placing the cask over a fire of shavings burning in a small *cresset* or brazier. Taking advantage of the softening staves, the cooper and his assistant drive successively smaller truss hoops over the staves at the open end, using the butt ends of their *trussing adzes*, until it is possible to put on an iron hoop the same size as the raising-up hoop. To ensure that the staves dry out and set rigidly in their new position, the *firing* is continued for about half an hour.

Chiming is the next operation: preparing the ends of the cask for the heads. With his adze the cooper first cuts a *chime* or bevel round the inner ends of the staves and follows it with a neat trim with his *topping plane*, which is curved to work round the cask end. This produces a platform on which to rest the *chiv*, a plane-like tool which cuts a broad, shallow channel across the inside of the staves about 2 in below the chime. The *croze*, a rather similar tool, can now be used to cut a narrow groove in this smooth channel for the head to fit in.

It is now safe to remove all but the two end hoops in order to *clean down* the cask, inside and outside. A *downright shave*, similar to a spokeshave with a slightly concave blade, is used on the outside, followed by a scraper called a *buzz*; an *inside shave* is used on the interior. Special attention is paid to the internal joints on which a curled-blade *round shave* is used, though some makers prefer a home-made flat steel scraper with a curved edge. Cleaning down is important because it minimises the danger of bacteria breeding on rough surfaces.

*Bunging* now involves the fitting of the bung bush. The cooper selects the stoutest stave for the bung hole and bores a 2 in hole in its centre with his *auger*, reaming it out to the desired size with a *taper auger*. The brass bush is then screwed in with a *dog*, which grips and turns it. (Wine and spirit casks have no bush as the brass would react unpleasantly with the contents.) Because the bung stave is subject to a lot of hammering it tends to crack rather often and Mr Swigoniak has a good number of them to repair.

The heads of small casks are made from three pieces of oak, those of large ones from four or more; the outer pieces are known as *cants*, the others as *middle pieces*, and they are pegged together with wooden dowels and caulked with lengths of Dutch salt-water rush. To find the size of a head, the cooper steps a pair of compasses round the head groove until by trial and error they fit six times – this gives him the required radius. The heads are cut out with a saw (allowing extra over the cants as they will shrink in the course of time) and then shaved smooth with yet another plane-like tool, the *swift*. In order to fit the head groove the head must be given a bevel or *basle* on each side, and this is done with another very sharp draw-knife, appropriately known as a *heading knife*. After the top basle has been cut, the circumference line is drawn again with the compasses and the edge carefully trimmed with the heading knife. These operations are done with the head pressed against the block by the cooper's chest, a somewhat dangerous posture; Mr Swigoniak prefers the continental method of holding it in a horse and keeping his chest clear! When the time comes to insert the heads, each end hoop is removed in turn and more rush is pressed into the grooves to make a good seal. A *chincing iron* – like a blunt chisel – helps with this.

Finally, the proper hoops are put on. Hoop iron is obtained in ready splayed lengths, but the cooper can hammer one edge out further if it is necessary to increase the splay. The ends are riveted together on the *bick*

*A cask head is fitted by removing the chime hoop and tapping the head into place from below with an angled rod inserted through the bung hole. A nail is used to give additional pull.*

*iron*, a tall T-shaped anvil with holes in the top, by overlapping the ends of the hoop above a hole and driving a cold rivet smartly through the mild steel. The hoops are hammered tight on to the cask with the aid of a *driver*, a wooden wedge whose steel tip is grooved to stay on the hoop edge. Small casks have only two hoops at each end, the *chime hoop* and the *bulge hoop* coming about one third of the way down the cask, but those over 36 gallons (barrel) capacity have another, narrower *quarter hoop* fitted between them. A fourth, the *pitch hoop*, is often put on very large casks.

All that remains is for the head to be branded with the brewery name, the chime painted to indicate the nature of the contents and then stamped with the cooper's mark – JS. 'If it should come back for repair, that is the man who repairs his own cask,' is an old rule of the trade quoted by Mr Swigoniak. As to the matter of output, he reckons that a man would do well to turn out two 36-gallon barrels in a day.

Not many realise how complex the cooper's craft is ('People mostly think you are a drunkard') but the traditional initiation of the young cooper who has completed his 'time' usually seems to be remembered.

*The brewery name is branded on the head of a finished cask. Notice the smoothly worked chime round it and the neat riveting of the hoops.*

Mr Swigoniak went through it in his turn: he was placed in a newly-fired cask and water, shavings and ashes were flung on him. Then he was rolled three times round the floor, and afterwards given a certificate and a pint of beer to aid recovery. Now the craft is so close to extinction (except in Scotland where the whisky distillers must still have wooden casks for maturing) that the occasional initiations of recent years have attracted a good deal of attention from the newspapers and television; they have become a rare item of folk lore.

What does a man do when he finds that the trade in which he's grown up and acquired his skill disappears before his eyes? It is one of the problems of our times that many a man has had to face, and some have been adaptable enough to find new ways of diversifying their abilities. Mr Swigoniak, like some other coopers, has turned his hand to a form of white coopering, making a range of garden tubs in various sizes and finishes that sell as fast as he can make them. He has adapted standard woodworking machinery for the speedier production of staves and heads, and so has managed to keep the craft going in a somewhat modified form; but of sad necessity he is among the last of his line.

# The glove knitter

As recently as the 1950s there still flourished in the busy market town of Ringwood one of the few English cottage industries to have survived into the mid-twentieth century: hand glove knitting. It may have had its roots in the small-scale textile production which was carried on here and there in the region, as in many other places, up to the early nineteenth century. Stockings are mentioned as a local product in 1780, and the Post Office Directory of 1847 says: 'There is a trade of some extent carried on in the manufacture of a peculiar kind of knitted woollen gloves and stockings; it employs about 90 hands.' This suggests that a good market existed despite the output of manufactured knitted goods from the Midlands, and further search in old directories (often a valuable source of information about trades) shows how the numbers employed in the work rose to 250 in 1855 and double that number by 1878. They were employed as outworkers by one Robert Cox. In later years, two local haberdashers and other firms in Dorchester, Blandford and Salisbury were the chief agents for gloves, and by the end of the Second World War, 800 women were said to have been making *Ringwood knits*, some at a considerable distance from the town.

The suggestion has been put forward that the industry started when a group of local women got together to devise their own special stitch, but this seems suspiciously like a later invention of local pride, and in any case there is nothing unusual about it. One writer in recent times has claimed that the stitch was a guarded secret, and if that was so a great many people were privy to it!

The knitting of Ringwood gloves on a commercial basis has now come to an end and most of the surviving knitters are advanced in years. One of the few still to be active in a small way is Rozanna Bursey, who was born in the town a few years before the First World War. Hers was a busy, if not hard, childhood: to be the eldest of eight children meant a lot of work and little play, and when her mother died Rozanna, then aged fifteen, was left with responsibility for the others, their ages ranging from nine months upwards. In due course she brought up five children of her own, by which time the knitting and sewing she had been taught at school had been put to good use. She became one of the glove knitters in 1940, at a time when there was a big demand for gloves for the armed forces, and she turned out a glove an evening, three pairs a week. The total weekly output during the war years is estimated to have been 3000 pairs.

The traditional Ringwood pattern is handed down from one knitter to another and Mrs Bursey learned it from a neighbour. These are its essentials, working on four needles:

**Main pattern** (produces the knot effect)
    2 rounds knit
    1 round knit 1, purl 1
    (Use an even number of stitches to keep
    purl stitches in line.)
**Dimensions in knots** (man's glove)
    Palm: 5 knots small hand, 6 knots large hand
    Thumb: 14 knots
    1st and 3rd fingers: 10 knots
    2nd finger: 11 knots
    Little finger: 7 knots

Variation is, of course, allowed for hand size.

As well as wool, gloves were also made in Liscord, a hard-wearing cotton yarn looking like silky cord which Mrs Bursey always used when working for local firms; it was supplied in bulk and had to be wound into balls. Four colours were popular: navy blue, grey, white (for police wear) and yellow (for riding use – it stands the wear of reins). Mrs Bursey liked knitting in the dark colours best in case her work got grubby from hands stained with housework, and she stuck to one size in ladies' and mens', preferring to make the latter.

For some time she made gloves for one of the local firms, then for one in Luton, and eventually for a London firm who complicated matters by requiring work to be done to a pattern they supplied. 'It took me a long time to figure it out,' she remembers. 'I used my own judgement, but they all passed, every one!' When Mrs Bursey began knitting she was paid 9d (4p) a pair, which gradually rose to 1/6d (7½p) and 2/10d (14p). But by that time the death knell of the craft had been sounded by the arrival of cheap Far-Eastern goods which could be sold for less than the local knitters were getting. By 1958, commercial production had come to an end and Mrs Bursey and others were able to continue only on a private basis.

Gloves being made for firms outside Ringwood were taken on Wednesday mornings to specified houses for cash payment and no doubt the knitters made collection days something of a social occasion. Those working a long way outside the town, rather than send work in by post, would make an effort to deliver it personally for the sake of keeping up their local links.

This outline is perhaps enough to indicate that it would be interesting to know more about the origins and organisation of a craft industry which is rapidly falling into obscurity, not least because so little is known about the development of knitting in its basic form; but the researchers seem to have neglected it and one of Ringwood's best-known manufactures, which has kept warm the hands of countless British servicemen from the Crimean War onwards, has yet to receive the attention it deserves.

# The hurdle maker

Panels of wattle hurdling are a popular, inexpensive form of garden fencing, particularly common in southern England, but how many people have ever seen them being made? Few, probably, for the hurdle maker's calling is one which takes him much of the time deep into the woods, where he generally works alone or just with a mate. Finding Cecil Bailey, then, needed determination and was only managed in the end by recruiting his small son as a guide. Five weeks elapsed between the author's first and second visits, and in that time he had seen no other person in the wood near Kings Somborne but his uncle, who was working an adjacent area, and the same son who came to play on Saturday mornings. In fact, the only person he ever does expect to see is someone from the local timber yard calling with a Land Rover from time to time to collect finished work. The life is a lonely one and has sometimes been known to make its followers reserved and slow of speech.

On a summer afternoon, with birds singing in the green depths of the hazel coppice and the scent of wood smoke rising from a fire of chippings, hurdle making seems a singularly pleasant occupation. But in the winter it looks less appealing, and Mr Bailey is there all year round, no matter what the weather, apart from his annual week's holiday. In one fortnight of the previous January he managed to get in only one-and-a-half days' work; the rest of the time he was obliged to sit through the rain in his little corrugated-iron shelter. Mr Bailey has the fit look of the outdoor man, but it is a demanding job physically and his hands are much scarred and calloused from splitting and weaving the hazel rods. In the summer his working day runs from 7 am to 5 pm with a half-hour break; in winter, from daybreak to dusk. But he does the job from choice, having tried farming and factory work and found that neither gave him the same sense of independence. His father, also a hurdle maker, encouraged Cecil to try the work, and after leaving school and spending some time learning under an old hand, he set up on his own. At that time, the early 1950s, he reckons there may have been as many as twenty makers busy in local woods; which makes an interesting footnote to a Forestry Commission survey of the same period which found that more men were employed in the hazel coppices of Hampshire than in any other county. However, the situation has changed since then and Mr Bailey thinks there are probably less than a dozen makers left in his area.

The liking of the hazel for the well-drained soil of the Hampshire down-lands attracted several kinds of underwood craftsmen in the past, but of them all – makers of sheep cribs, crate rods, gate hurdles – only the wattle hurdle makers remain. They all depended on the willing way in which the hazel regenerates when cut right back to the stool, or base: the result is vigorous growth of numerous new shoots and the creation of coppice woodland, frequently dense, with thick clumps of long straight rods reaching up to the light. These are left to grow according to the require-ments of the worker – eight or nine years' growth is about right for Mr Bailey – but if not cut regularly they will be poor. One can walk through a hazel coppice and trace the hurdle maker's progress by the lengthening new shoots from the stools, while low mounds of old trimmings show where the hurdles were actually made.

Each year the hurdle maker buys an area of coppice sufficient for his estimated needs. Three acres is enough for Mr Bailey and for this he pays according to the quality and density of the hazel. The annual sale of underwood used to be something of a local occasion at one time. Lots were sold in the early autumn at a meeting in the club room of the Crown Inn, and each purchaser was required to have a bondsman, since payment was not made until cutting finished in the spring when the lots were measured. Around Kings Somborne the coppices are parcelled out in areas known as *burls*, which do not correspond to exact acreages. It needs a practised eye to spot the boundary of a burl – a line of thin stumps cut off at about three feet high.

Before Mr Bailey can begin making his hurdles he must cut a consider-able quantity of the growing rods, which he does first thing each day with his *cutting hook*, a curved hand bill. It used to be the practice for hurdle makers to cut all the rods in winter when the sap is down and leave them to season, but they are easier to work when newly-cut. They should not be much more than about $1\frac{1}{2}$ in thick. After trimming off twigs and foliage, the rods are dragged to the working site where most of them are split right down their entire length of 8 or 10 ft. This is done with another bill, the *splitting hook*, which has a hooked blade. If there is no convenient fork at the narrow end of the rod, the hook is started in carefully at the side and worked down with a rapid twisting motion of the tip, which opens the split with a characteristic rending sound. Splitting

*A hurdle begins when selected uprights, called sails, are knocked into the mould. Behind the maker is his rail, notched as a cutting guide, and also used to support split hazel rods ready for weaving.*

is a skill which seems to excite admiration, and some unwary observers have even tried it for themselves. Mr Bailey remembers a lady reporter from a London paper who wrote him up some years ago: 'Came down here one day and tried to split the rods out, and cut her finger and had to go to the doctor and have two stitches.' Such temerity is not quickly forgotten.

Hurdles are made on a *mould*, which is a stout curved length of split beech about 7 ft long, anchored in the ground by pegs and wire. It is generally supposed that if made flat, hurdles would become slack as they dried out; whereas made slightly curved, they tend to tighten up. Drilled into the mould are nine holes about 9 in apart to support the uprights, called *sails*, and pronounced with a 'z' in this part of the country. The maker stands on the convex side of the hurdle as he works, with his back to his *rail*, a horizontal pole about 10 ft long which supports the rods ready to hand for weaving. The rail has a stop cut at one end of it and a series of notches along its length, against which rods can be measured when cutting sails for hurdles of 3 ft, 4 ft, 5 ft and 6 ft height, plus an allowance of 4 in for the points. A stout stump set up against the rail serves as a chopping block when making the points with a *sailing hook*.

Construction of a hurdle begins with the nine sails being firmly knocked into the mould with a mallet, which is just a handy wooden cudgel. The centre and outside sails are round rods (the latter somewhat stouter) and the remainder are split ones. When the weaving starts, it goes at such a steady pace that one might think there was little to it, but it needs a strong wrist and a good deal of experience. Moreover, there is a structural sequence to be followed – it varies somewhat from area to area. Mr Bailey first *ties-in* the *bottom heathers*, six or seven small round rods which are placed between successive sails and woven from left to right and round the outside sail, producing a braided edge. The two outermost bottom heathers are twisted twice round the end sails and bent up at an angle, locking the base up tightly. After this, the body of the hurdle is built up with split rods, the first ones being introduced in a sequence which levels up the weave. As each one is brought round the end sails it is twisted and bent, a special trick of the hurdle maker to ensure that there are no outside fibres to crack. (Thatchers do the same thing with their spars.)

The hurdle grows upwards, and as it does so, first feet, then knees, and finally the mallet, are used to ensure a tightly-packed weave; knee pads are cut from old rubber boots. The white split sides of the rods generally all face outwards, and it is possible to obtain a pleasing effect by varying them. Sometimes the hurdle displays a tendency to twist during making, and Mr Bailey uses his *trigger* – a short forked hazel prop – to support it. A simple measuring rod is used to check overall width.

When the weave has reached within a foot of the top at one side it is worked in a staggered slope up to 3 in from the top at the other, ready for a section similar to the base to be made. First comes the *johnny spur*, a round rod whose end is started at the highest point, twisted round the end sail and tucked in five or six courses below. It is followed by two split rods, the first one being twisted twice round the end sail and tucked behind it like the johnny spur. The two final rods are round ones, the *starber* and the *finisher*, which braid the top of the hurdle and make it secure. All that remains is trimming, for which the hurdle is either laid flat on the ground or rested on two short, upright posts just in front of the mould. Yet another variety of bill, the *nugging hook*, with a short cutting edge on one side of the blade, is used, and a stout length of waste wood is held under the end being trimmed to prevent damage to the panel. Then the hurdle joins the stack growing nearby, and, as Mr Bailey says, 'The best part of the job is seeing them on the heap.'

The width of wattle hurdles is a standard 6 ft, so the price varies accor-

*Checking the width of a hurdle. The small section of round rods at the base has been worked in such a way as to lock it up tightly; a similar procedure is followed for the top edge.*

ding to the height. The whole of Mr Bailey's output, along with that from most of the local makers, is taken by a firm of timber merchants in the village, an arrangement which enables him to maintain a steady income all year round. The hurdles go far afield, to Sussex, Gloucestershire, and even to the Channel Islands where they are used as windbreaks for the early flowers. If treated properly (creosoted when dried out and nailed, not wired, to strong posts) they ought to give ten to fifteen years' service.

Wattle hurdles were found useful in a number of ways in the past. Up to the seventeenth century they were used with a clay coating as wattle-and-daub walling for huts and timber-framed structures. Thatched roofs often rested on panels of hurdling placed on the rafters, and they occasionally come to light when stripping roofs long undisturbed. In earthwork fortifications, hurdling was used to form breastworks and revetments. Most familiar of all were the hurdles used for folding sheep, especially at lambing time when shelter was needed; they were made with a slot in the weave so they could be carried on a pole over the shepherd's shoulder. Continuously-woven hurdle fences were once popular and are still to be met with here and there; their texture makes a pleasing background to

*A finished hurdle and the tools used in its construction.*
*(1) Cutting hook: for getting the hazel (2) Splitting hook (3) Sailing hook:*
*points the uprights (4) Mallet: beats down the weave (5) Measuring rod (6)*
*Nugging hook, used with (7) Trimming piece: placed under waste ends when*
*trimming (8) Trigger: prop to support the hurdle.*

garden borders which can be much more attractive than factory-made
timber panels.

The steady demand for hurdles suggests that the craft is far from
dying, but the real danger is that few young men are taking it up, and the
lonely working conditions could be the reason for this. A possible problem
in the future may be shortage of raw material. With the decline in use of
underwood, fewer acres of coppice are being sold for cutting, and, in
consequence, owners are looking for better returns from their land. Many
coppices have been cleared in recent years and in one more way the
familiar appearance of the countryside is being changed.

# The rake maker

For a man who leads an unobtrusive life, Ernest Sims of Pamber End must be known by reputation to a good many people. Over the years he has been written about in newspapers and magazines, interviewed on radio and television, recorded on film and referred to in many of the books dealing with rural crafts. But then, he is probably the last man in southern England to be making the wooden rakes which were once in such demand in the hayfields. A very few others may still be at work in Wales and the north of England, turning out rakes of a pattern suited to regional conditions, but for all of them the market is greatly reduced since the days when large quantities were needed and expected to have only a short life. Despite the pace of agricultural change, many rake makers were busy well into the present century, particularly in areas like the Kennet valley of Berkshire, for example, where the raw materials grow freely; and there was some casual rake making in the woodyards of country estates where there has always been a tradition of self-sufficiency. Mr Sims can remember the time when there were actually enough makers to support a short-lived Rake and Snead Makers' Union. (A snead is a scythe handle – Mr Sims made them also until after the last war.)

There is a history of rake making in the Sims family stretching back for well over two hundred years, and Ernest continued it by joining his father when he left school in 1908 at the age of thirteen. Demand then was enough to provide employment for an uncle and two other men as well, though as the family also did some farming one cannot be sure just how large their output was. Mr Sim's two sons in turn stayed at the job with him until 1953, but he now works alone and only part-time.

Between October and the end of March Mr Sims makes expeditions with bill and handsaw to Brimpton for his raw materials – ash, birch or willow for the handles, Dutch willow for the heads and black willow for the teeth. But demand having fallen off, he no longer needs to go annually and he can get enough wood in one winter to last him two years. It is

*With the rake head firmly gripped in a simple bench clamp, two holes are drilled for attachment of the handle. The angle of these holes determines the working efficiency of the rake.*

sawn up prior to seasoning, into lengths of 30 in for heads and teeth and 7 ft for handles, then *rinded* by taking off three strips of bark with a bill-hook. This allows it to season more gradually than if completely stripped and prevents it from going *coaly* and brittle. The wood is then left under cover for at least six months.

Adjacent to the cottage where he lives and in which he was born, are the two thatched sheds in which Mr Sims carries on his work. One contains a steam chest and a setting brake, the other an upright brake, or shaving vice. Outside are two or three other pieces of equipment. In his father's day most of the work was done outdoors, but now Mr Sims generally works inside. However, a sunny day in spring or summer may find him busy at one of the benches near his well-stocked garden, a rake tied to the fence like some defiant symbol of the old order while the traffic races past down the road to Basingstoke.

*The rake teeth are pointed with deft strokes of the draw-knife while the head rests in brackets on the shaving brake. The latter is basically a large clamp which also holds the rake handles while they are being rounded.*

As a rake is made in three parts (in batches) we can look at each in turn, beginning with the handle. The seasoned pole is trimmed to about 6 ft 9 in, and *flatted off* with a short axe at one end for about 20 in of opposite sides – this will be the head end. Many of the poles are far from being straight, and have to be corrected by steaming before going any further. The steam chest is a box about 8 ft long and 2 ft square, connected by piping to an old domestic copper, and holds some three dozen handles. After twenty minutes inside they are soft enough for straightening in the *setting brake*, which is nothing more than two stout pegs projecting from an upright beam, against which the handles can be strained as required. Then they go across to the other workshop, a little room crowded with accumulated paraphernalia of rake making and shared with sacks of potatoes and a somnolent cat. The chief feature here is a large wooden *shaving brake* which fills the window by the door; in essence it is a rectangular frame supporting a wooden vice opened by a lever and held shut by weights suspended on a wire. In this vice the handle is gripped to be smoothed, first with a draw-knife which removes bark and knots, then with a *stail engine* or rounder. This is a rotary plane working very much like a big pencil sharpener, with two handles by which it is turned round and along the rake handle to smooth it. Putting the handle next on one of his small benches or *horses* where it is held by a wooden hook worked by a foot clamp, Mr Sims makes a sawcut about 20 in long in the flattened end. As the sawcut proceeds, he puts a small wedge in the cut to hold it open, and, when he has gone far enough, nails a strip of tin round the handle to stop it splitting further.

To shape the heads, the lengths of willow are first quartered on the chopping block and then reduced with a draw-knife to a section about 2 in by $1\frac{1}{2}$ in. Another horse is now used for boring teeth holes and the head is kept steady on it by wedges pressing against wooden stops. A notched stick is used as a spacing guide and the holes made with a brace and auger bit. These days Mr Sims works to 'thirteen gauge', but in the past he would make rakes with 14, 15 or 18 teeth. (As a youngster it was this job that he used to find the hardest.)

In making the teeth, the lengths of black willow are first sawn down to 6 in long, then split into pegs and rounded on an ingenious device, the *tine former*. This is yet another horse, one end widened as a seat, while through the other passes a length of steel tubing held by a collar. The upper end is sharpened, and as the rough pegs are tapped through by a mallet they are quickly and easily shaped.

Assembly of a rake begins with tining the head, which for this purpose is held in an engineer's vice. With a cobbler's hammer Mr Sims taps the end of a tine to flatten it slightly, dips it in water and hammers it into the hole with the flattened sides along the grain; this, he claims will reduce the risk of splitting. Once furnished with a row of tines, the head at last begins to look purposeful but it is not finished yet. The rough ends of the teeth projecting through the head are trimmed off with an axe and a neat chamfer cut at both ends. Then the back of the head is smoothed off with the draw-knife. Using a little wedge called a *tipstick*, the head is held in the brake with teeth outwards, so that they can be sharpened with the draw-knife, first one side, then the other. If any roughness remains on a tooth it is removed with a tiny hooked shave, a little tool which Mr Sims treasures, for it would probably be impossible to get a replacement. Back on the horse used for boring, the head is wedged in a different position and two further holes are made, about five pegs apart, to receive the split ends of the handle; the angle at which these holes are made will determine the position of the head, and on this will depend the rake's

*The rake maker's tools.*

*(1) Round shave: removes bark from handles (2) Draw-knife: shapes head, sharpens teeth, cleans up head (3) Saw: divides end of handle, cuts teeth to size (4) Bushman's saw: cuts raw materials (5) Notched spacing guide: used when making teeth holes (6) Hooked shave: cleans up teeth (7) Hammer: for knocking in teeth (8) Axe: for quartering heads (9) Bill: cuts raw materials, rinds handles (10) Brace: holes for teeth and handles (11) Axe: splits teeth, trims heads (12) Stail engine: rounds handles (13) Mallet: knocks teeth through tine former.*

gathering efficiency. After a little trimming, the handle ends are pushed into the holes where they are nailed and the ends cut off. The rake is finished – a light, serviceable piece of craftsmanship that is a tribute to homespun ingenuity and its maker's practised eye.

Mr Sims sells his rakes for a sum most people would think a very small return for the time it takes to make each one – the best part of an hour and a half, he reckons. In his grandfather's day they sold for $4\frac{1}{2}$d (2p) each, and just before the First World War for $8\frac{1}{2}$d (4p) each. Some he sells to callers at his home, but most, by a curious irony, are taken by a firm in Birmingham. His output in a fairly active week may be between six and seven dozen. It is pleasant to be able to add that, despite the publicity his work has brought him, Mr Sims is quite unaffected by it and remains a contented man of strong faith and simple needs.

# The sedge plaiter

When it was founded during the First World War, the Women's Institute movement was much concerned about the economic problems facing its members in many country areas. It was believed that with suitable guidance women could find new ways of making a useful contribution to their family income and so bring fresh hope to situations often depressed by miserably low agricultural wages. To this end, opportunities were sought for building up rural industries in which a small scale of operation would be no disadvantage, and, being essentially hand crafts, there would be little competition to fear. Various crafts were tried, and as they could mostly be carried on in the home using simple equipment and inexpensive materials, promoting them meant little more than demonstrations and instruction. As it turned out, the financial rewards were rather small but an enthusiasm for craft work was engendered and remains to this day, with emphasis upon its enjoyment as a pleasant and worthwhile pastime. Two crafts achieved some degree of success in Hampshire: skin glove making at Netley and sedge plaiting in various parts of the Test valley.

Old photographs show that the plaiting was thriving at Micheldever and Leckford as early as 1919, for in a picture taken at the latter place fifteen ladies are to be seen holding examples of their work, which includes mats of various sizes and baskets. Things were well set up at Micheldever where there was a Rush and Sedge Industry run by W.I. members with its own organisation. With the aid of husbands and sons, sedge was cut at Hunton near Stoke Charity and at Itchen Abbas, while supplies of rushes came from Fordingbridge. A Stoke Charity lady who gave up the work in 1948 remembers practising both sedge and rush work, and how she wove the rushes over a suitable former to achieve the desired shape. It is apparent from various sources that a wide variety of products was attempted in sedge, such as dog and log baskets, Moses baskets, shopping baskets of various patterns, workmen's lunch baskets with hinged lids retained by the handle, hassocks and mats. As the plait for mats was sewn up on edge, it was possible for a pleasing spiral motif to be inserted.

To what extent sedge plaiting may have thrived in the county earlier, is uncertain. Rush plaiting is known to be an ancient craft, once carried on in many parts of Britain, so it is reasonable to assume that sedge also has long been used; indeed, it would be surprising if such an abundant raw material had not been exploited along the county's river valleys.

The moving spirit in the plaiting revival was Miss W.G. Bedington of Longstock, who was still demonstrating the craft at the end of the Second World War, and it was at one such demonstration at this time that Beatrice Dobson was inspired to take it up. Although there were then still enough plaiters to be able to put on displays at agricultural shows she is now one of the last to be active. She had a few lessons from Miss Bedington and has been plaiting ever since.

Longparish, where Mrs Dobson lives, is one of the most delightful of the thatched villages sprinkled along the Test Valley and her cottage with its fruitful garden is not far from the river banks where the sedge grows so profusely. Her husband, Harold, is a river keeper and the obvious person to be pressed into service for cutting and carting it. Much of the sedge is burned off by the keepers for the sake of tidiness during the March winds and this results in clean, strong growth during the summer. It costs nothing but the labour of cutting and after permission has been sought Mr Dobson gets to work with his sickle in July, when the leaf tips are starting to turn brown. He brings home perhaps twenty roped bundles.

Mrs Dobson then gets busy, cleaning out the rubbish and dead pieces and tying handfuls with string on a line to dry. This takes two or three days, bringing the sedge in at nights and avoiding the bleaching effect of direct sunlight. When thoroughly dry, it is hung up in a shed until wanted. Although green when cut, the sedge gradually turns pinky-brown with age; it has a pleasant aroma and is altogether a very attractive material to handle and use.

The quantity of sedge required for the day's work must be prepared in advance by laying it overnight on the lawn to dampen, or if the weather is dry, by soaking in the rainwater butt for twenty minutes. Afterwards it is rolled in a towel or piece of sacking to dry off surplus moisture – it is undesirable for the sedge to become sodden. The actual plaiting is begun by tying a small bunch to a piece of string which is looped over a hook; Mrs Dobson has one in the wall beside her living room fireplace, where she can stand or sit as the work proceeds. With the plait thus held at one end, the work can be kept taut and a neat, even plait is the result. Mrs Dobson usually works a seven-strand plait. The method of working is the same as for a simple three-strand plait (which she sometimes uses for table mats), that is, the strands are turned inwards, four and three on each

*From bundles of dried river sedge (back) the maker produces a seven-strand plait which is sewn up in a coil (front) to make attractive baskets. Handles go right round the undersides. The big log basket is double-walled for strength.*

side alternately. Strands of varying length are added as the plaiting goes on and are inserted underneath the right-hand side. Thus there are no obvious joints in the work and all the ends can be trimmed off on the back.

At an output of about one yard an hour, seven-strand plaiting is rather slow work and a calm temperament is needed to enjoy doing it. Perhaps that is why, when Mrs Dobson is sometimes asked to teach the craft to others, few of them stick at it. But she finds it restful and relaxing. About twelve yards of plait are needed to make a shopping basket and like all the other products it is made up from a coil. A neat start is important since there is a tendency for the first turn or two to spring open. The plait is sewn up on the wrong side, edge to edge, using a curved upholsterer's needle and working on a square of wood to protect the table. Untreated raffia is used for sewing because it blends in well with the sedge.

To make a circular shopping basket, the plait is turned up at an angle from the base to form the sides. A length of plait for the handle is passed twice underneath the basket and the loops are sewn together above; they are separated underneath to spread the support. A long flower basket is made by bending up a large coil and sewing in two smaller ones at the ends as gussets. Log baskets have to withstand heavy wear and are made double, a basket within a basket. Added strength is given by attaching two pairs of loop handles at right angles, running right underneath the base; sometimes they are bound with raffia to make a more comfortable grip.

Mrs Dobson works regularly at her plaiting for about two hours a day and it takes her an evening to make up a shopping basket. In six months she may turn out some twenty baskets, most of them 'shoppers' which sell as fast as they are made. There is no need to advertise and, indeed, she often has to turn customers away. With such a ready market for goods which look well and wear well it seems a pity that few are willing to persevere at the craft. Raw material costs nothing and the only equipment needed is a needle and scissors and nimble fingers.

# The thatching spar maker

Among the materials which the thatcher requires, and uses in some quantity, are the thin pointed *spars* of hazel wood, which are known by many other names in different parts of the country. They are variously used to hold down the underthatch, to secure the edges of long-straw work, to form the diamond-work on the ridge, or, bent like hairpins, to peg the top coat to the underthatch. In the days before combine-harvesters, when hay and corn ricks were also thatched and rickyards had a neat, personalised air that the baler has since destroyed, even greater quantities of spars were required. Farm hands were often set to making them in bad weather, when other barn work was in abeyance, so they would be ready for the time when the thatcher was called in after harvest, or they themselves were required to finish off the ricks. When farm labour was plentiful, a number of rural crafts were practised as a matter of course by men who were not specialised craftsmen; it was part of the old self-sufficiency of the countryside.

Spar making has necessarily been closely linked with thatching, the fortunes of one being dependent on the other, but the returns from this monotonous work are so slender that it is invariably met with as a part-time occupation carried on by those connected with the timber trade, such as foresters or underwood workers. Years ago, when much more thatching was done, spar making was sometimes relied on by the elderly or incapacitated as a small source of income that would help to keep them out of that most dreaded institution, the workhouse.

Two brothers, George and Arthur Hatch, work industriously at spar making in a little workshop close to the New Forest at Copythorne where George, the elder, has been busy for over forty years. Even before he left school he was helping out in the family timber business, giving a hand with the book-keeping for which, with more schooling, he was better equipped than his father; at fourteen he started full-time. It was not long afterwards that the man his father supplied with wood for making spars

*A small adze, forged from an old hammer, is used to start the splits when making spars. An upright peg fastened to the yew chopping block assists in opening the splits.*

was caught burning the stock to keep warm, and that was when George took up spar making. It took him about a year to become proficient and not only did he work a six-day week from 7.30 in the morning to 6 in the evening, but he had to begin and round off the day by feeding the horses. But those were depression times when you were lucky to have regular work of any sort and you had to seize (and make) your opportunities. Arthur, who is some years younger than his brother, came into timber work and spar making in due course and the two men now spend perhaps a third of their time at it – long mornings at the weekend, sometimes evenings, sometimes a whole day; the rest of the time they work in a local timber yard.

Spar making is one of the few survivors of that once-large group of underwood crafts which relied on coppice-grown hazel for their raw material. It is a shrub with a tendency to throw out straight, whippy stems and regular cutting encourages the habit. For the spar maker, growth of about eight years is adequate and the Hatch brothers have two spells of cutting in local coppices: at the beginning of October and early in the

*There is a certain knack even in pointing thatching spars. When bent and twisted by the thatcher they will become an effective means of pinning down the thatch.*

New Year. They work with axe and billhook, cutting the rods to working length on the spot; a sample piece 26 in long is kept handy for checking. Stout lengths that might otherwise split are sawn up in a *sawing horse*, a simple cradle with two X frames. At one time they also made spars of 32 in and 36 in length for rick thatching, but now they only turn out one size unless otherwise asked. The hazel lengths, tied up with baler twine in bundles about a foot in diameter, are brought back by tractor and trailer.

The brothers' workshop is a wooden hut some 20 ft long and half as wide, where they sit on either side of an iron stove, sharing its warmth as as they work. If it seems remarkable to find two men sharing the labour of such a simple craft, with George doing the splitting and Arthur the pointing, they can demonstrate the output possible in this way: about 4000 spars in an eight-hour day with short breaks. They make an impressive stack. (The brothers know of a Sussex spar maker and his wife who share the work in the same way.)

After any knots have been trimmed off with a billhook, the rods are ready for splitting. A rather curious tool is used for this, a 16 oz hammer

183

*Spars are counted out into this simple holder before being bundled. The wood-man's grip, a cable attached to two levers, is wrapped round the bundle while it is done up.*

which a local blacksmith has forged into a small adze; George got the idea for doing it this way from his early experience splitting chestnut poles for fencing. Resting the rod on his chopping block, a yew log about 2 ft tall, he starts the adze into its side at one end; then, as soon as the split is wide enough, he levers it further open by means of an old billhook blade fastened upright on the side of the block. Thus the blade supplies leverage while the adze guides the direction of the split. A leather pad on the left knee affords useful protection. The yew block, although chosen for its hardness, has to be renewed every year. Depending on the thickness of the hazel, it can be split into four, six, eight, ten or even more spars, and as George wields his adze in one hand the bundle grows in the other. Ideally, he likes to split 'eights' out of rods $1\frac{1}{4}$ in – $1\frac{1}{2}$ in in diameter. From time to time an armful of spars is passed to Arthur, who sits on the remains of an old chair against the side of the shed, a sack folded across his lap, smoking a well-used pipe. His only piece of equipment is a small, curved billhook that was once his father's and which he keeps razor-sharp. With it, he puts a long point on each end of the spars, three strokes to each; though if the season is advanced and the rods have got hard through long keeping, five are required.

The spars are done up in bundles of about 250 by first placing them in a pair of rests that are simply short pieces of plank with uprights set into them at a slight angle; then the bundle is squeezed tight with a *woodman's grip*, an ingenious device made from two battens about 3 ft long and 2 in square, joined at 6 in from one end by some 4 ft 6 in of steel cable. This cable is looped right round the spars and the arms pressed down on each side and levered against the underneath. The arms are kept in place by kneeling on them while the bundle is tied up with two lengths of galvanised wire. Finished spars are sold to at least half a dozen thatchers, one from as far away as Reading, and may be used on roofs even more distant. (The chips too, used to be sold for use in laundries, when old-fashioned flat-irons were heated on slow-burning stoves.)

George and Arthur Hatch know that their work is secure as long as thatching flourishes; but who will be making the spars when they give up? Probably the thatchers themselves, possibly the hurdle makers, though some thatchers prefer not to approach them for fear of being supplied with spars made from waste. The fact is, that a shortage of makers is already being felt and it looks as though one more small band of country-side workers may soon be no more.

# The wheelwright

Men who can make wheels are now few and far between, their exacting craft an almost total victim to the inexorable stride of technology. One wheelwright's shop is still working at Houghton, in Hampshire, where Ken Potter and his assistant Alfred Bowles keep the old skills alive, and one would have to look far and wide to find the next one in southern England. Yet three generations back, wheelwrights were among the commoner craftsmen to be met with in town and countryside alike and road transport was heavily dependent upon them. A hundred years ago there were at least eight busy within a few miles of Houghton and four were still to be found in 1915.

Mr Potter was born in an age when the vast majority of road vehicles – carts, carriages, wagons and omnibuses – moved on wooden wheels. A war was being fought in South Africa that could no more have been prosecuted without wheelwrights than it could without saddlers and farriers, and it looked as though hand-made wheels would be needed as long as horses were. It must have seemed a steady sort of job to take up, bearing in mind that Mr Potter's father and grandfather before him were also wheelwrights – his father was a Somerset man who settled in Houghton in 1910 after a time spent moving about the south of England as a journeyman wheelwright. But the writing had been on the wall for some time, though few cared to believe it. The motorcar, still thought by many to be no more than a novelty, was showing its paces, the bicycle had introduced a radically new kind of wheel, and the development of iron hubs and woodworking machinery meant that even wooden wheels were subject to factory production.

Only a few years after starting work, Mr Potter went off to the First World War. Three years later he came back to his old job and in another two the wheelwrighting trade had virtually died. The great transport revolution of this century was gaining power and wheelwrights everywhere fell on lean times or were forced to look for other work. While his father struggled on, Mr Potter tried working as a wheelwright in an Andover engineering firm for less than a shilling (5p) an hour, but finding that kind of life uncongenial gave it up and went into the building trade in the London area. In 1927 he came back to the village and established himself as a carpenter, doing local work and making kitchen furniture for the trade. For a wheelwright to turn carpenter must have been fairly common and Mr Potter remembers how it used to be said in his father's day that, 'A bad wheelwright would make a good carpenter.' He also acted as local undertaker, following family tradition and the practice of many country wheelwrights. (It gave them a particularly close association with their neighbours in the days when death was still a community affair, and Mr Potter's conversation about the Houghton area is interspersed with re-collection of funerals from one house and another.)

Few wheelwrights survived those difficult years. Horse-drawn vehicles became scarcer as they were replaced by motors in one trade after another, and farmers gave up their heavy wagons for light trailers, often because it was easier to replace than repair them. Then, in 1966, having reached an age by which most men would have long since retired, Mr Potter was asked to repair a wheel; and then another. Wondering if the tide was turning, he placed an advertisement in a riding magazine and found that there was indeed a growing demand for wheel repairs from driving enthusiasts and collectors. Soon he was discovered by the press and television and a great volume of work began to pour in; now he has to quote delivery dates several months ahead.

Mr Potter's story shows how a craft may survive in order to meet a specialised demand. When his father first came to the village there was plenty of work to keep him busy, making and repairing the wheels, carts and wagons that were used locally. Now it is the better-off person with a pony and a paddock, who has discovered the pleasures of slow motion and wants a trap doing up, or the purchaser of an old gipsy caravan, who constitute the typical customer. Museums too, often need wheels re-building, and so does the Army, strangely enough, for its ceremonial gun-carriages. It is really rather remarkable how many gigs, phaetons, rallicars, caravans and carriages survive – far more than there are suitable horses and capable drivers to handle them. So it looks as though there will always be work for a few wheelwrights who will perhaps achieve the status of antique restorers in due course!

It was mentioned that wheelwrighting is exacting work, and a skill that takes years to acquire cannot be treated justly in a page or two. The reader seeking detail can be referred to no finer account of the craft than that written by George Sturt of Farnham in Surrey, who in 1884 inherited a wheelwright's business when he was only just out of school and in 1920 retired with an extensive knowledge of all sides of it. Sturt was gifted as a writer and was able to describe not only the work of the shop and the selection of raw materials but also the character of his workmen in a way that makes his book a classic epitome of the old traditional craftsmanship.

There are five principal parts to a wheel: the *hub* (also *nave* or *stock*), the *spokes*, the *felloes* (pronounced 'fellies'), the *tyre* and the *box*. They must be made from well-seasoned materials, accurately cut and fitted. Elm (which does not readily split) is the preferred timber for hubs and Mr Potter buys it in the round and leaves it to season for six or seven years, boring holes through the blocks to assist the process. He likes to keep a stock of his principal timbers always seasoning. When ready for use, the hubs are turned on the lathe, the holes being temporarily filled for this purpose. Cutting the mortises which will receive the spoke tenons must be done with great care, after their positions have been found by stepping a pair of compasses around the hub, and then drawing round a tenon as a template. There is always an even number of spokes, two to a felloe. First, three auger holes are made, then the remaining waste is removed by chiselling, the corners being cleaned with a *buzz* (or *bruzz*), a heavy square chisel with an L-section edge. The cutting of the mortises will determine the *dish* or slope of the spokes and the angle is checked by trying a spoke in the mortise against a *spoke set gauge* screwed into the hub centre. It will be noticed that in many large wheels the spokes are staggered alternately to front and rear of the hub, which is a means of partly compensating for the thinness of wood between mortises, and of spreading support for the rim. Iron *stock hoops* are nailed on the hub ends to minimise the danger of splitting when the spokes are driven in.

Oak heartwood when it can be got, otherwise ash, is used for spokes, cleft rather than sawn to avoid weakening the grain. The spokes are shaped with draw-knife, spokeshave and file and a tenon is cut on the foot to fit the hub mortise. Then, with the hub clamped in a long, open-framed *wheel stool* the spokes are driven home with a sledge hammer, each one being tested against the gauge to see that it is at exactly the right angle. The *shoulders* of the tongues are marked off with a scriber or *spoke trammel* rotated from the hub, and round tongues are cut which will fit into the felloes; a sawcut is made halfway down each for subsequent wedging.

Large felloes are cut from elm, smaller ones from oak or ash, after the curves of *back* and *bosom* have been marked out with a pencil fastened to the end of an adjustable bench-mounted compass arm. Two holes are cut right through each to receive the spoke tongues and another is made in each end for wooden dowels to prevent the felloes moving. The felloe ends are cut to the wheel's radius. The problem of getting two spokes angled away from each other into the felloe holes is solved by the use of

*The felloes of a wheel are particularly subject to hard wear and decay, and replacing them is one of the commonest jobs a wheelwright is called on to do. These newly-cut ones are being tried for size before further shaping.*

a *spoke dog*, a strong lever and hook device which cramps the spokes slightly together as the felloe is tapped onto the tongues. When assembled, a wedge is driven down the sawcut of each tongue to hold it tight, and the circumference of the wheel is cleaned off with draw-knife and smoothing plane.

In larger wheelwrights' shops, such as George Sturt's, there were men who specialised in making and fitting tyres and other ironwork, but the wheelwright usually needs to call on the services of a blacksmith at this stage. Mr Potter is lucky to have as a neighbour, Mr Burt, the blacksmith who lives a few doors along the road, and two or three times a month they get together for a day of tyring. Mr Burt's father worked at the same forge before him and to find two village craftsmen still active within yards of each other is distinctly uncommon these days.

First, the exact circumference of the rim must be found by running round it a *traveller*, a metal disc of known circumference pivoting in a handle. Strip iron is then curved in a bending machine and the ends forged together, making a hoop about ¾ in smaller than the wheel. Typical tyres range from 2 in × ½ in to 3½ in × ⅝ in.

Wheels are saved up for tyring in batches, until the wind is in the right quarter – though that is a purely local precaution to avoid subjecting neighbouring cottages to the smoke. It is quite an exciting operation. The tyres are laid on concrete blocks in Mr Burt's yard and old rubber tyres stacked round them to burn with a fierce crackling blaze that creates terrific heat and dense clouds of black smoke. Meanwhile, the wheels are stacked near the *tyring platform* and the first one is got ready by clamping it down to the big iron disc while the necessary tools and buckets of water are laid out for quick use.

When the first tyre has reached a dull red heat, and so expanded just sufficiently, it is lifted out of the inferno and carried quickly to the platform and eased over the wheel. It is helped into position with claw-ended levers called *tyre dogs* and knocked down with a sledge hammer. Smoke and smell rise as the wood chars or bursts into flames and for a few moments there is frenzied activity as the men hop round the platform getting the tyre on. Immediately it is right, buckets of water are poured over to cool the tyre and it contracts amid a cloud of steam, hissing and cracking as the wheel locks up tight. It is a rare and fascinating thing to see and often attracts a little knot of interested spectators.

There are no nails, screws or glue used in making a wheel: its strength lies in accurately made joints and the cramping action of the tyre. The few nails put through the tyre are to counter any tendency to creep and also the shrinkage that almost inevitably occurs in the course of time. Farm wagons used sometimes to be stood in the duckpond for an hour or two as an antidote, and now when a tyre has got very slack it can be *cut and shut:* removed from the wheel, a small section cut out, re-forged and replaced as described.

Many of the wheels Mr Potter handles are re-tyred with a channel for rubber tyres. He has a lever-operated wall-mounted device which squeezes the rubber and presses it into the channel; the ends need no joining.

Before the wheel can run on its axle, the hub has to be bored out and a cylindrical iron bearing or *box* inserted. A self-centring hand-turned *boxing engine* is clamped onto the hub and the cutter adjusted to make a hole slightly oversize for the box. When the box is in place, the wheel is hung on an arm and hardwood wedges are knocked into the end grain of the hub so as to tighten it against the box; at the same time its centring is checked by rotating against a marker on the ground. Sometimes the wedges can be spotted in the hub of an old wheel that has shrunk slightly. Finally, the wheel receives four coats of lead paint.

Just as the customers have changed, so have some of the old ways – and not without reason. Mr Potter recalls that cutting out a pair of ash

*Tyring a wheel is an exciting business, calling for good teamwork as the hot tyre is levered and tapped into place. The wheel, firmly clamped to the iron tyring platform, has a tendency to catch fire. This channelled tyre will later be given a solid rubber insert.*

wagon shafts meant sawing some 25 ft by hand; now he can do it on his bandsaw in a matter of minutes. The same tool replaces the bowsaw for cutting out felloes. Another machine he finds especially useful is his mortiser, which he uses for quick clean cutting of smaller hub mortises. With an auger attachment it will bore spoke tongue holes in felloes and, with a paired hollow auger, shape the tongues themselves. In the workshop there are also a saw bench, a planer and a lathe, the latter fortunately not needing the assistance of an apprentice to turn a huge driving wheel, of the sort that was common in old wheelwright's shops. All these machines are driven by a system of underfloor line shafts and belting turned by an elderly 6 h.p. Lister engine.

Many customers at the Houghton workshop want not just wheels but entire vehicles renovating and Mr Potter and Mr Bowles are equally practised at stripping, re-building and re-painting items as different as trotting cars and showmen's caravans. Outside help is brought in to cope with the specialised work of upholstering and the paint lining of wheels and bodies. One shed is set apart for painting work. Another is used as a vehicle store where there are usually some interesting items to be seen; others may be parked in the yard, alongside the stacks of old tyres, shafts and useful bits and pieces that accumulate in such a business.

To go into the main building, however, is to step into an old-fashioned country workshop of the kind that survives all too rarely. It is a roomy place that looks as though it has grown out of three large sheds put together. One part houses the woodworking machines, another is the main working area. On the street side of this is a long, low window with overlapping panes, through which the late afternoon sun shines on a rack full of auger bits and other tools; a bench runs the whole length of the window. Against two other walls are stacked wheels waiting for repair, for painting and for tyring. In the centre stands a wheel bench on which much of the repair work is done, while in the rafters above are stored lengths of timber and old patterns for wagon parts. The floor is earthen. In this room, probably little changed in the course of sixty years, survives the genuine atmosphere of country craftsmanship created by men who enjoy and take pride in their work. It was here, a few years ago, that the Worshipful Company of Wheelwrights came to make a film record of the wheelwright's craft to celebrate their Tercentenary, and they could have chosen no better place.

# VANISHED CRAFTS

# The makers of nickies
## and sieve hoops

Wanderers along the byways of local history occasionally come across a reference to some activity or other that intrigues because it is left unexplained. An example is the making of *nickies*, a New Forest occupation mentioned in passing by one or two writers but apparently never described. When finally elucidated it turned out to be a very simple craft, no longer practised, but worth recording here since it could probably be paralleled in other areas. The author's informant was Joseph Mansbridge who has spent his whole life in or close to Marchwood.

First, however, it must be explained that a nickie is nothing more mysterious than a little prepared bundle of kindling wood of a kind that must have been made in the Forest for centuries past. Mr Mansbridge first saw them when he was very young, shortly after the beginning of the century, and he knows that members of his family were making them before that. Like his father, he pursued until retirement a way of life shared between farming and timber dealing, mostly in underwood products such as stakes and poles. Underwood working results in a lot of surplus brushwood which can be put to little use and is generally burned, but the nickie makers could use just about all of it. While cutting was going on in the winter months, it was collected and tied up with hazel withies in big double armfuls (mostly hazel and birch) and brought into the woodyard to dry; the bundles were appropriately known as *longtails*. They were piled up in stacks the size of hayricks, the top being sloped to run the rain off, and left for three or four months to dry thoroughly.

The nickies were very quickly and easily made by folding up, concertina-wise, a handful of the brushwood about 9 in long, and tying it with a green withy (the countryman's tie noted elsewhere in these pages; the withy is twisted to prevent the fibres breaking). Then the ends of the nickie were trimmed on the chopping block with a billhook. Bundles of twenty-five were made up with another stout withy while held between the legs.

Mr Mansbridge recalls that nickies were mostly made by elderly women, for some of whom it was an important source of income, while men would only make them to help out their womenfolk. The women worked at it for as long as ten and twelve hours a day, making anything from 400 to 1000. 'I knew one old lady that would tie a thousand, and my aunt told me she'd be working and singing those Sankey hymns all the time.' At 3d (just over 1p) a hundred, it was not much of a living, but it was clearly welcome employment and doubtless gossip and hymn-singing helped to break the monotony.

Bundles of nickies were sold at 4d (2p) each or 1s.4d. (7p) for four – that is, a hundred nickies, twenty-five in each bundle. They were regularly ordered by hospitals, churches, shops and businesses and Mr Mansbridge supplied many thousands. Southampton was the limit of his deliveries. The demand for nickies finally ceased as the Second World War began, partly because of the increased availability of alternative forms of heating which required no kindling, and partly because of a sudden need for unskilled labour for more urgent purposes.

Another activity which ought not to go unmentioned was the making of sieve hoops, carried on until just after the war by a firm of timber merchants at West Dean in which Charles East (now retired) was a partner. He used regularly to help out with making the hoops and so remembers the work well, which is fortunate since he may be among the last who do.

It all began with his grandfather setting up in business at Hyde Abbey Sawmill, Winchester, in the early 1870s, where he specialised in two rather unusual lines, cutting beech and other hardwoods into brush blocks (the blocks into which the bristles are set) and making sieve hoops. Grandfather took the opportunity of getting closer to the source of his timber by moving to West Dean on the Wiltshire border in 1890, and here the firm has remained, its output now diversified, but still making great quantities of brush blocks. Mr East started to work in the sawmill during the First World War, putting in an hour or two after school and more on Saturdays; he joined full time when he left school in 1920, just after the 48-hour week was introduced. (Before then the men had worked 10 hours longer for 4d an hour.) His week's work brought him only 10 shillings (50p), but at least in those days it was possible to buy a suit for that sum!

The best wood for most sieve hoops was beech, though for garden sieves, ash and elm were also acceptable. It was all home-grown timber and mostly got from no more than ten miles away; the important thing about it was that it should have good planing qualities. In the sawmill it was converted to long slats about $\frac{5}{16}$ in thick and then put to dry for

*Planed and lapped slats were steamed and rolled up in bundles, then left to set in hoops like those in the front. Finished hoops were used for tambourines as well as for all kinds of domestic and garden sieves.*

between one and three weeks (depending on the time of year) in the drying sheds used for brush blocks.

The next stage of the work was carried on in an upstairs workshop in a corner of the timber yard, where the slats were planed and *lapped*, that is, one end was given a long chamfer so as to overlap smoothly when the sieve was made up. Every slat was planed smooth on both sides by hand; and if that seems something of a labour, Mr East recalls that the firm once erected a split pale fence three miles long, round a local estate and all the 60,000 pales used were planed by hand. After planing followed lapping, when the slats were held firm, a dozen at a time, under the clamp of a *horse*. The maker sat on this long stool facing the stack of slats, his feet pressing against the bar of the clamp to hold them tight, and rapidly sliced off the chamfers with his draw-knife. As each one was done the clamp was slackened and the slat removed. To keep the two processes running level, two men would be employed on planing and one on lapping, and a daily output of up to four gross could be achieved, more if the slats were small. Some rough hoops were entirely cut and lapped by sawing.

Having been planed and lapped, the slats had to be steamed and set in hoop form. The steaming box, in which the slats spent about twenty minutes, was operated from the yard's steam engine. When pliable, the slats were rolled up quite tight by a windlass device and placed in wooden setting rings which held six of the larger ones, more of the smaller; here they were left for a time before a couple of tacks were hammered in to hold the roll and it was removed. Two or three times a week finished hoops were packed in sacks and trundled along to the station on a hand truck for despatch to manufacturers in London and Bristol.

Hoops for various kinds of sieve were made in some twenty sizes, while another dozen sizes of narrow hoop were made for tambourines. Although they turned out this unusual item for so many years the firm made only a tiny profit from it, and when the source of steam for the steam box was finally replaced by a diesel engine in 1946 it was seen as an appropriate moment to end production.

# Bibliography

GENERAL

Arnold, J. *Shell Book of Country Crafts*, 1968
Edlin, H. L. *Woodland Crafts in Britain*, 1949 republished 1973
FitzRandolph, H. E., Hay, M. D. and Jones, A. M. *The Rural Industries of England and Wales* 4 vols., 1926-7
Hartley, D. *Made in England*, 4th ed. 1974
Jenkins, J. G. *Traditional Country Craftsmen*, 1965
Salaman, R. A. *Dictionary of Tools*, 1975
Woods, K. S. *Rural Crafts of England*, 1949 republished 1975

THE BASKET MAKER
Wright, D. *Baskets and Basketry*, 1972

THE BLACKSMITH
Hogg, G. *Hammer and Tongs*, 1964

THE BOATBUILDER
Salaman, R. A. op.cit. Article 'Shipwright'

THE STONEMASON
Jenkins, J. G. op. cit. Chapter V

THE TAILOR
Whife, A. A. *The Art of Garment Making* (no date)

THE THATCHER
Rural Industries Bureau *The Thatcher's Craft*, 1961

THE WOOD TURNER
Stokes, G. *Modern Woodturning*, 1973

THE BOWYER
Bilson, E. *Modern Archery*, 1956

THE FARRIER
Hogg, G. op. cit.

*Bibliography*

THE FLY DRESSER
Veniard, J. *Fly Dressers' Guide*, 4th ed. 1970

THE SADDLER
Hasluck, P. N. *Saddlery and Harness Making*, 1904 reprinted 1962

THE SAILMAKER
Bowker, R. M. and Budd, S. A. *Make Your Own Sails*, revised ed. 1975

THE BOOKBINDER
Burdett, E. *The Craft of Bookbinding*, 1975

THE FURNITURE MAKER
Bradshaw, A. E. *Handmade Woodwork of the Twentieth Century*, 1962

THE POTTER
Billington, D. M. *The Technique of Pottery*, revised by Colbeck, J., 1974

THE BRICK MOULDER
Woodforde, J. *Bricks to Build a House*, 1976

THE BROOM SQUIRE
Jenkins, J. G. op. cit. Chapter II

THE COOPER
Elkington, G. *The Cooper's Company and Craft*, 1933
Salaman, R. A. op. cit. Article 'Cooper'

THE HURDLE MAKER
Jenkins, J. G. op. cit. Chapter II

THE WHEELWRIGHT
Salaman, R. A. op. cit. Articles 'Wheelwright', 'Wheelwright's Equipment'
Sturt, G. *The Wheelwright's Shop*, 1923

# Index